Modern

Young People

*A collection of humorous royalty-free
dramatic sketches for teen-agers*

By John Murray

Publishers   PLAYS, INC.   *Boston*

Library of Congress Cataloging in Publication Data

Murray, John, 1923–
  Modern monologues for young people.

  Summary: Twenty-four short monologues dramatizing in lighthearted fashion the ups and downs of life as seen by today's young people.
  [1. Monologues. [1. Monologues] I. Title.
PN4305.M6M75   1982   812 .54   82-5331
  ISBN 0-8238-0255-8   AACR2

Contents

1

Home Sweet Home Computer

❦

> BILL LISNER *enters right. He carries a rectangular object, about the size of a portable television set—a "computer"—which he places on a chair downstage. The face of the computer is away from the audience.* BILL *calls off right.*

Hey, Ann, I'm home. Come into the living room. (*Turns left, calls off*) Mary, Bert, come downstairs. I want to show you something. (*Cocks his head*) I don't care whether you have a cake in the oven, Ann. (*Proudly*) I have something here that will change our lives! (*Impatiently; turns as Ann enters*) No, no, I haven't hired a maid.

(*Turns as children enter*) I'm glad you kids could tear yourselves away from the TV. (*He points to computer.*) There it is. A bright new way of living in a world of technology. A Crab Apple Home Computer! (*Pauses*) Why do

3

we need a computer? Ann, I'm surprised at you! Do you realize that this little terminal will balance our bank statements, pay our bills, choose our menus, watch our investments, teach us algebra, electrical mechanics, and ancient history? And best of all, it will teach us foreign languages— French, Italian, Arabic, and Tasmanian. (*Pauses; with hands on hips*) Well, of course it's important to learn Tasmanian, Mary! I *am* being serious, Bert. (*Pauses; more annoyed*) No, it doesn't play the latest Rolling Stones album, Mary. You can't have everything!

Ann, will you forget the cake in the oven? The Crab Apple computer will give you a perfect cake every time. Here, I'll show you. (*He pantomimes punching computer keys.*) Now, what kind of cake are you baking? . . . Apple cinnamon surprise? O.K. Here are the ingredients. (*He squints at computer, reads.*) "3 cups of flour, 2 cups of brown sugar, one cup of cooking oil" — (*Looks up*) What's that, Ann? Your mother never used cooking oil in her cake recipes? Well, I've tasted your mother's cooking, and I think a computer would help her a lot.

(*He continues to read*) "Bake in a 350° oven for 30 minutes" — (*Looks up*) What do you mean, we have a slow oven? (*He sighs.*) Ann, you have to use a little ingenuity. Bake the confounded thing at 375° for 45 minutes! (*Reading*) "Remove cake from the oven, and (*He frowns*) — Four score and seven years ago, our fathers brought forth upon this continent — " (*Hesitates*) Gee, I must have gotten the cake program confused with the American history program. (*He smiles uneasily.*) Of course, a little adjustment will take care of that.

All right — forget the cake. We'll try a little accounting. Let's find out about our current bank balance. (*He pulls a slip of paper from his pocket, and then starts punching keys on computer.*) Our last statement showed a balance of $71.43. Now, I deposited $500.00 last week. Ann, you deposited the $25.00 present from your Aunt Frances and $13.49 from your bowling league award dinner. Then we spent $200.00 for Mary's braces, and we had an electric bill, telephone bill, the oil bill, and insurance, and mortgage, and car payment, and the unpaid balance of our federal taxes. O.K. That does it. (*He punches key on computer with flourish.*) Our present bank balance is — (*In disbelief*) 4 million dollars? (*He shakes his head; perplexed.*) But I don't understand it. (*Pointedly*) Ann, are you sure you didn't make any other bank deposits? (*Pauses*) I am *not* being facetious! (*Thoughtfully*) I might have pressed a few zeros too many. Maybe the hardware input is reacting to the software output. (*Pauses*) It's very important, Mary. You must always watch your hardware and software.

(*Sheepishly*) The cost of the computer? Well, Ann, it *is* new and things are always more expensive when they first come on the market, and we'll be the first family on the block to own one! (*Soberly*) Yes, the cost. (*Nervously*) Well, it was a trifle over $2,100, and — (*Alarmed*) Quick, Mary, get your mother a glass of water! I think she's going to faint. (*Holds arms out*) Please brace yourself, Ann. After all, we'll own the thing in 60 months, and — (*Angrily*) it will *not* be obsolete by that time, Bert!

Oh, there are all sorts of programs, Ann. I got the works! (*Punches keys again*) Here's one you'll like. It will help you choose the proper cosmetics and the right shades of clothing to suit your personality and mood. (*He punches keys.*) All we have to do is put a few pertinent facts about you into the computer. (*Pauses*) Now, I'd call your complexion a little sallow. (*Looks up*) All right, Ann. You're fair-complexioned. (*Pushes key*) The shape of your face? Well, I guess it's pear-shaped (*Quickly*) — I mean, heart-shaped. (*Laughs nervously*) Your chin is pointed — patrician, I mean — and you have a swan-like neck. (*Smiles in satisfaction, then frowns; defensively*) That's poetic, Ann! I meant nothing personal. (*He reads computer.*) There! The program is appearing on the screen. (*Reading*) "Apply a bright tinge of Chantilly rouge to each cheekbone; green eye shadow and a carmine lipstick worked into a bow-shaped pattern; a delicate powder to cover the wrinkles" (*Looks up*) — Sorry, Ann! I meant to say laugh lines! — "and wear a high-collared blouse to minimize the over-long neck." (*Defensively*) I didn't say your neck was too long! The Crab Apple Home Computer said it!

All right, we'll forget the beauty lesson and get down to important business — wise investments! (*With glee*) I just know this wonderful computer will pay for itself in no time. (*He presses several keys.*) There it is! (*Reading*) "Guaranteed investments for the coming fiscal year should be Hawaiian Islands gold mines and the Alaskan wheat market." (*He shakes his head.*) I don't know about that. I never heard of Hawaiian gold mines, and I guess there's not too much wheat grown in Alaska. (*He shrugs.*) It must be an old program.

Give me the manual, Bert. (*Holds out hand*) I must have made a computer registration error — or something. Let's just forget about investments for now. (*Looks through manual*) Here's something for the kids. (*Reading*) "How to compute Babe Ruth's lifetime batting average." (*He frowns in disbelief*) What do you mean, who's Babe Ruth? What is this young generation coming to? (*Pauses*) No, Mary, Babe Ruth isn't a candy bar! (*Calming himself*) All right. We'll put the batting averages aside. This family doesn't have any athletic interests, it seems.

(*Smiling broadly*) Ann, you're going to love this. Are you ready? (*Stops smiling, as if he's received a negative response; sarcastically*) Well, don't be so enthusiastic! (*Becomes excited again*) Really, you'll love it. It's a computerized routine of daily housework to add pleasure to your leisure time. (*Reading*) "Monday — 9:00 AM. Change the bed linen, do the laundry. 11:00 AM. Shop for groceries, buy hardware for home improvement projects. 2:00 PM. Weed the garden and plant new flowers. 3:00 PM. Clean the basement, write letters to friends and relatives, plan recreation for the children, inaugurate a new cultural program for the neighborhood. 4:00 PM. Prepare dinner. Consult the Crab Apple computer for such simple dishes as carbonade à la Flamande, shrimp à la suede, bordelaise. 5:00 PM. Spend a relaxed period following the computerized beauty hints in chin and neck massage — " (*He pauses; annoyed*) Ann, I can't help it if the computer keeps mentioning your neck. (*Reading*) "Wear a casual gown of pink and magenta for the evening, and — " (*Sighs heavily*) Yes, Ann, I know you have red hair. (*Pause*) Pink and magenta would clash? Well, don't blame the computer because you came from a red-haired family. (*Reading*) "7:00 PM. Plan an interesting evening playing bridge or discussing world events with neighbors." (*He gestures.*) There it is. An active day for the modern housewife.

I don't appreciate that remark, Ann. What makes you think you'd be too exhausted after following the simple daily routine? (*Pauses*) What do you mean, you have no time to follow political events? Well, someone has to keep an eye on those people in Washington, and the computer will do it for you.

(*Impressed*) This computer is simply amazing. Here's a program that covers income taxes, stabilization, upward mobility, foreign loans, international crises, and — (*Looks closely at computer*) Drat! There's the Gettysburg Address again. We simply have to iron out the bugs in this thing.

(*Looks up*) No, Ann, you don't smell anything burning. The Crab Apple Home Computer is completely shock-proof, waterproof, fireproof, and — (*Suddenly*) your cake? Uh-oh! (*Sniffs the air*) Something *is* burning! (*Frantically*) Mary, quick! Get a pan of water and help your mother douse the fire!

(*Suddenly*) Hey, wait a minute — why are we so excited? We can get the fire department with our home computer. Bert, set the fire department number into the program. (*Rubs hands together*) That's great. (*He reads computer.*) "Shall not perish from the earth." (*Quickly*) Forget the computer, Bert — get to the telephone. (*He sighs.*) Well, Abe Lincoln never had an apple cinnamon surprise in his oven.

(*He turns*) What's that, Ann? (*Pauses*) Charred to a crisp? Now, stop looking at me like that. After all, we can't stand in the path of technology. (*Throws hands up*) All right, so I'll find a program to reactivate a burned cake!

(*Brightly*) Cheer up, everyone. We'll have a happier life in a day or two, when we've mastered the computer. (*He turns, begins to walk right, then stops, turns.*) Where am I going? Why, I'm going to take a little walk in this bright, new, modern world. And I'm headed for the drugstore, for an old-fashioned bottle of aspirin! (*He holds his head, exits right.*)

THE END

2

Space Flight to Saturn

> MRS. MARTIN ELLIS, *a middle-aged woman,*
> *enters right. She carries a small suitcase. There*
> *is a chair down center.*

(*Excitedly*) Well, here we are, Martin. The Interstellar Spaceport, at last. I was sure we'd be late for our flight. That air traffic is dreadful! Why, it's getting worse every century. And the way those teen-agers flit around in their space cars. (*Nostalgically*) Oh, for the good old days when 10,000 miles an hour was considered a sensible speed. (*She shakes her head, sets case down.*) I don't know what the universe is coming to. You checked our luggage—good! I hope you monitored our robot to make sure that it gets on our flight to Saturn. . . .Well, you know how so many of those robots act — so unconcerned! And don't forget our last flight, when our things were routed to some dreadful place called Atlantic City!

By the way, I hope you didn't overtip the robot. (*Cocks head*) A million dollars? (*Satisfied*) Yes, that seems like a fair tip to me.

(*Excitedly*) I can hardly wait to see our daughter Stellarina again! (*Frowning*) I just can't figure out why she left immediately after the wedding reception. (*Distastefully*) I suppose her husband couldn't wait to return to Saturn. (*She clucks disapproval.*) There's something about that young man. Why, Stellarina could have had her pick of any fellow at the space academy. (*She smiles.*) Now, that young chap from Mars was such a nice boy—with that purple curly hair, and that simply divine blue eye in the center of his forehead.

(*Pause, then indignantly*) I am *not* interfering in Stellarina's married life! Why do you think we're making this flight to Saturn, anyway? (*Wrings hands*) It's just that I get so worried, having her live way out there without any modern conveniences. She space-phoned the other day and told me she actually has to prepare her own food tablets. Disgraceful! And her husband has a lot of nerve, saying that he operates three plutonium fields. Hmph! More likely he manages a few worthless gold mines!

(*She cocks her head.*)

Oh! They're announcing our space flight to Saturn! (*Points*) There's the conveyor belt to launching pad 273, but that robot is heading for the Jupiter station with our luggage. (*She calls.*) You with the metal head! Our luggage belongs on the Saturn flight. . . . (*She stamps angrily.*) Martin, did you see the indignant look that robot gave me?. . . .Well, he would have given me an indignant look if he had a face. Oh, those robots!

(*She smiles.*) Do you like my corsage, Martin? Your sister Eritrea sent it to me as a going-away gift. Yes, it's a moon lotus, although I don't like the way it keeps snapping at the collar of my spacesuit!

(*She points to chair.*)

Well, here are our seats. (*She sits, sighs.*) It'll be so good to relax for five light years. I think you should have asked your boss for an additional three light years of vacation. . . . Well, we could have spent a little more time with Stellarina. . . .What do you mean, her husband might object? Why, we'll be no bother at all. I'll be able to help Stellarina with the housework—pressing buttons, managing the domestic robots, and all those other dreadfully trying things.

(*Cocks head*) The captain is speaking on the thought-transmittal reactivator. Sounds as if he's from mid-west Jupiter. He's telling us to adjust our interplanetary space helmets. I just hate to put that thing on my head! It will ruin my deactivated, radium-sensitive home permanent.

(*Points out toward audience; pleased*) Oh, good. There's a telethought machine. I hope they show a movie. These super-saver flights always feature some old films like *The Venus Godfather* or *Gidget Goes To Mars.*

(*In disapproving tone*) Martin, will you look at that flight attendant! Really! The clothes that our young people are wearing these days are just shocking. Why, her metal skirt barely covers her knees! . . . I am not being old-fashioned! (*Proudly*) In my day, a liberated woman always dressed sensibly. . . .Oh, dear. She's heading this way. (*She smiles falsely, then addresses flight attendant.*)

No, my dear, we won't need a plastic adapter, a rubber connector for the air track, or a filter bag. We're seasoned

12

space travelers, I assure you. . . . What? . . . You were considering our age? (*Indignantly*) Well, I'll have you know that I've barely seen 150 summers, and—(*Looks off*) Why, she's gone!

What do you think of that, Martin? I suppose they feel they can insult passengers on a super-saver flight. Well, Interstellar Space Flights will hear a thing about that!

There's our robot again. (*Shocked*) And he's serving the meal! I didn't realize there was such a shortage of labor. (*Eagerly; addresses robot*) Oh, you have our dinner? How nice! Well, I'm not really hungry, but I think I'll have a chicken-checkered tablet. . . .Yes, you might add some gravy. (*Points*) That's the green pill. . . .Mashed potatoes? The red pill, of course. (*Points again*) What's that perfectly delicious-looking little pearl pill—vanilla ice cream?. . .Oh, no—I'm on a diet. (*She takes several pills, swallows them.*) Ah, perfectly delectable! Send my compliments to the chef! (*Looks at Martin*)

Martin, what are you doing, bending over the aisle like that?. . .You're talking to the young woman in the next seat? (*Firmly*) Martin, you must be careful about fellow passengers these days. . . .She's traveling to a word-processing secretarial convention, is she?. . .And she's very excited? (*Haughtily*) I can imagine!. . .And you think she's attractive? Well, I'd be attractive, too, if you bought me a platinum, neon-transfixed wig. . . .Well, of course she's wearing a wig. (*She nods.*) A woman can just tell. (*She braces herself in the seat.*)

We're off the launching pad! How exciting! (*She points right.*) What a panoramic scene! That bright light over there must be the planet Pluto. . . .What? A space-platform

13

Burger King? (*Clucks disapproval*) What's that interesting object that just sailed by?. . .A garbage disposal unit launched from planet Earth! It's simply terrible the way those people litter the universe!

Look at all those beautiful moons! Why, the ancient songwriters would have had a marvelous time with all these moons to write about. (*She sighs, leans back in chair.*)

Space travel is so relaxing! (*Suddenly*) Oh, Martin, I hope you left a telenote for the milkman robot not to leave any capsules for the next five light years. . . .Ah, that's good. And you didn't forget to call the telethought company and the teleview newsboy, did you?. . .I am *not* being over-cautious. (*Upset*) Oh, I can see I should have attended to everything myself before we left. The captain is speaking again. (*Upset*) Martin, we're running into a star shower!. . .Well, you know how nervous I get in storms—and I remember that asteroid fall when we visited your parents. What a nightmare! I simply cannot understand why they insist upon living in Albany. There are so many retirement communes only 5,000,000 miles away.

I do hope the neighbors will look after our house while we're away. I asked them to run the jet-distilled water pump every day. And what about the space cars—did you lock the garage? . . .Well, you know what's been happening in the neighborhood. These are wild, dreadful times.

Did I just hear the captain say that we have a transfused airhose leakage?. . .We'll have to make an unscheduled landing in Venus and board another plane? Oh, no! . . . Well, I don't have a thing to wear in Venus!

We'll have to get our luggage transferred to the new flight. (*She beckons.*) Young man—er-young woman—er-young

We'll have to get our luggage transferred to the new flight. (*She beckons.*) Young man—er—young woman—er—young robot. (*She turns to Martin.*) It's impossible to tell. (*To robot*) Yes, you, robot. Will you kindly get our luggage? (*Pause*) Well, you were given precise instructions to put them on the Saturn flight. . . .What? You thought we programmed Sacramento? My lovely things are enroute to California? (*She turns.*) Oh, Martin, what are we going to do?

We're descending on the landing pad—and I suppose we'll have to go through space customs. They'll want to see our passports for the Saturn flight. . . .(*In dread*) What? Oh, no, Martin, don't tell me that! (*In disbelief*) You— you packed our passports in the luggage? And it's in Sacramento! We'll have to take the first flight to Earth! (*She sobs.*)

Stellarina will be so disappointed. (*She clenches her fists.*) It's all her husband's fault—settling in Saturn. Well, I'll tell him a thing or two—if we ever get there. His ears will burn, all right—all four of them! (*She stands, nods emphatically, exits right.*)

THE END

3

Even a Child Can Do It

> PAUL GALBRAITH, *a young husband, enters.*
> *He fans his face with his hat. His jacket is*
> *slung over his shoulders, his shirt collar is*
> *open, and his tie is loose. The scene is the*
> *Galbraith living room. There is a chair*
> *onstage.*

Hi, Alice. How are things? . . . Hot? I'll say. It's been up over ninety all day, and the air conditioning at the office broke down. Funny how that thing always manages to conk out on the hottest day of the year.

Listen, I want a nice big tub of ice water. . . . How long? Alice, I'm going to sleep in that tub all night.

What's that big crate doing here in the living room? (*He examines carton, then brightens and throws his hat and coat on the chair.*) The chaise longue that we ordered for the sun porch? Why, I almost forgot about it. (*He rubs hands together.*) This is my lucky day. Those

16

big roomy foam rubber cushions! Those floating-on-air inner springs! Let me at it.

Sure I know how to assemble it. The guy at Star Furniture Mart said that it was so simple even a child could do it. . . . O. K., Alice, forget the remarks. I'll put the chair together and I won't need any help—or suggestions. Just give me a hand with the box.

(*He tugs at box.*) Gosh, it's packed pretty tight. Well, hold one end and I'll grab the other. Now, we'll pull. (*He tugs at box.*) That's the girl. I—I think it moved and—hold it tight! (*He falls backwards onto floor.*)

Why did you let it go? (*He stands and rubs back.*) Well, it's out of the box, anyway. . . . And leave that envelope alone. Why sure, they're the screws and nuts and bolts and things. Of course they have to go some place. Here, let me look at the parts. (*He rubs his chin and muses.*) Yes, yes, I have it doped out. Simple as ABC. Just bring me my tools. I won't need much—just a screw driver, a wrench, a soldering iron, three drills . . . yes, two metal clamps . . . no, no glue. It's not that kind of job.

Now let's see—I'll just take a look at these instructions, but I don't really need them. (*He picks up roll of paper and begins to unroll it. It gets longer and longer, and he stares at the paper, astonished, as he pulls it out.*) A real blueprint, isn't it?

Oh, thanks, Alice—just put them down over there. . . . Yes, these are the instructions. I guess they have to go into detail for some people who aren't handy with tools. Now, let's see. (*He reads.*) "Release the sprockets (A) until they reach direct alignment with hooped ratchets (B). Then—"

Now, just a minute. I have to figure out the sprockets

and ratchets first. . . . Well, I haven't messed with sprockets and ratchets in years, and a fellow can get pretty rusty. (*He touches a part.*) What's this little gimmick? A ratchet? No, it looks more like a sprocket to me. Well, let's fasten them together and see what happens. (*He adjusts bolts and stands back.*)

Well, it's beginning to look like a chaise longue, I guess—but what about that sag in the middle? Yes, a fellow's back would be on the floor. (*Impatiently*) All right! We'll reverse the whole thing. (*Pointing*) *Those* are the sprockets and *those* are the ratchets. . . . What's the next step?

(*He reads.*) "Place bearing spindle (C) and right axle brace (D) at direct angles with sprockets and ratchets. See diagram 3." (*He scratches head.*) Oh, no! Those sprockets and ratchets are back again. (*Sighs*) Well, a bearing spindle shouldn't be hard to find. (*He stoops and arranges miscellaneous parts.*) There must be a hundred parts on the floor. . . . Well, maybe they sent us *too* many parts. Stores can make mistakes, you know. (*He picks up a piece.*) That's the bearing spindle, I think. (*He assembles piece.*) Yes, I know, Alice. It still sags in the middle. Now, perhaps I should crawl under the thing and make some adjustments. . . . (*He lies on floor, waves his arms and legs wildly.*)

Help, Alice! Get this thing off me! Those sprockets are sharp. (*He pushes at the chaise longue and rises to his feet, shaking his head.*) Yes, the whole thing just caved in. Well, we might as well start all over again. . . .

Yes, I know a child can assemble it—but the man didn't say the child should have a degree in mechanical engineering! Maybe I should forget about the framework for now. If I were to spread the foam rubber cushions out on the floor and—O. K., Alice. I'll try it again.

(*He reads.*) "Bolts—Nuts—Washers—Spindles—Ratchets—Sprockets—Adapters—Pressure Deflector—" What's that last thing? A pressure deflector. . . . Of course it's important. That's why the whole thing fell apart. (*Impatiently*) Everybody knows you can't forget to deflect the pressure!

(*He rubs his forehead.*) All right, I'm sorry if I lost my temper. . . . I apologize. It's the heat, Alice. It's really getting me. Maybe I should forget the whole thing until after dinner and—no, I did *not* intend to leave everything on the floor. . . . O. K., so you cleaned today. Of course I'll tidy up. . . . And don't pout like that. (*Patiently*) Let's continue with the *simple* instructions!

(*He reads.*) "If ratchet and spindle do not turn easily—see Diagram 4-C—lubricate bearings with squeegee grease." Aha! That's the whole trouble. We haven't used squeegee grease. (*Points*) There it is—they sent a big tube of it. (*He removes cap, places tube against bearing and squeezes.*)

That's funny. It must be stuck or something . . . Yes, a bobby pin will do the trick. (*He takes bobby pin, inserts it into head of tube.*) There, I think we'll get the squeegee grease now. (*He presses tube vigorously.*) Oops—it slipped!

Oh, Alice, I'm terribly sorry—all over your new white dress, too. . . .Well, the grease should wash out, and—your face? Well, it won't hurt your complexion—much. Here, let me get the grease on the bearing before it gets temperamental again. (*He presses tube against bearing.*) Good,

good! It's going to work. See, it's disappearing through that little slot—(*He peers through slot.*)

Wait a minute! Quick, get a damp cloth. . . . Yes, before it soaks into the rug!

Well, don't worry about it, Alice. The squeegee grease is gone, anyway. (*He throws tube aside.*) Well, maybe I can salvage enough grease off the rug to lubricate the bearings and things. And there's a big blob on your forehead. (*He rubs his finger across her forehead, applies grease to bearing.*) Thank you, Alice. (*He turns a few more bolts.*) There—that about does it. (*He steps back to admire his work.*)

It looks like a fine chaise longue. . . . Yes, I think we're ready for the cushions.

What do you mean, it doesn't look very sturdy to you? Why, the salesman said it would support four hundred pounds. (*He places cushions on chaise longue, stretches, and smiles blissfully.*)

Yes, I sure am ready to relax. It was worth all the work. And they were right. Anyone can assemble it. . . . It will be a pleasure to try it. (*As he talks, he sits on the chaise longue, which collapses. He falls to the floor.*)

Help, Alice! Get me out of here. Take that ratchet out of my leg. All right—take the *sprocket* out of my leg! This is no time to be technical. (*He rises and rubs his bruised body.*)

Oh, my aching back! And look at my pants! Yes, the ratchet went right through the knee. . . . Yes, the whole chair is twisted.

Hand me that telephone. (*He takes phone and dials a number.*) I'll give those people a piece of my mind.

Hello? Star Furniture Mart? Well, this is Paul Galbraith. . . . Galbraith. G-A-L—what difference does it make how I spell it? I ordered a chaise longue. . . . Yes, that's right. (*Between clenched teeth*) The Easy-to-Assemble chaise longue! Well, I can't do it. . . . Oh, you're so right. Even a child can assemble it. Ha, ha!

(*Loudly*) Well, I want you to send a child right out here to put this ridiculous thing together. . . . Yes, yes, I know about the ratchets and spindles. One of them is sticking into my leg right now. . . . Yes, send someone tonight. Better send some more squeegee grease, too. Just in case! (*He sighs heavily.*)

Do I want to relax? (*Loudly*) Mister, I'm ready to collapse! (*He slams phone on receiver and lumbers off stage.*)

THE END

4

Bargain Day

> LAURA GRANT, *an attractive housewife, enters right. She clutches her purse as she turns impatiently and gestures to her friend. The scene is a large department store.*

Come on, Flo. Everything will be sold out before we get there. What? Yes, of course I know it's only nine o'clock, but this is the biggest sweater sale of the year. If they really do have all those cashmeres at only $39.95— still pretty expensive, you say? Oh, honestly, Flo, you sound just like George.

My dear, you should have heard him. He went into a perfect tantrum the minute I mentioned going to another sale. He finally calmed down a little when I told him it was only sweaters. . . . No, he doesn't. George doesn't know a thing about cashmeres—thank goodness. But he's so unreasonable about sales. He keeps remembering the last time I went out on a bargain day and bought that electric water softener. . . .

Yes, well how was I to know our water wasn't hard? Why do they sell water softeners in a city where nobody needs them? They *don't* sell them, you say? That's why they had the sale. Well, maybe, Flo—I never thought of that.

(*Points*) See—just look at that mob. I told you. Every woman in town must have sweaters on her mind. I knew we should have come earlier. (*She sighs.*) Well, we might as well jump right in and—pardon me, madame. (*She elbows through the crowd.*) Excuse me—excuse me. (*Glares*) Well, I certainly did get here before you did!

At least we're inside the store. Now to find the sweater counter. Let's ask that man at the information desk. (*She walks forward.*) Pardon me. I'd like to see someone in sweaters—er—I'd like to see something in sweaters. Can you tell me where the sweater counter— Oh, this isn't the information desk? The complaint department? Oh, I never come here until *after* I've made my purchases. (*She smiles sweetly.*) I—I'll see you later. Goodbye. (*She turns.*) Such a nice man! And so sympathetic, too. (*She sighs ecstatically.*) Oh, Flo, look at that divine desk with the book shelf on top. Yes, the one in mahogany. Chippendale? I'm not quite sure. One is bow-legged and one is knock-kneed, but it's always so hard to remember. (*She examines price card.*) $249.99! Imagine that! (*She drops card.*) No! I promised George I'd stick to sweaters—and that's that. But wouldn't the desk look lovely in the sun room? Well, we call it the sun room although it's on the west side and it never gets any light until sunset and— (*She straightens with determination.*) Let's find the sweaters!

Over there. . . . that must be the counter. My goodness, the people are three deep. Oh, there's an adorable pink sweater. I—I want it. Yes, that's the one—the lady's holding it.

Excuse me, madame, but I'd like to see *that* sweater and— Oh, you've already bought it? Waiting for it to be wrapped? (*Coldly*) Very well, if you saw it *first!* (*She turns.*) Can you imagine that, Flo? That dreadful woman bought the pink sweater. Of course, she isn't the pink sweater type, and I think she bought it out of spite.

I—I can't keep my eyes off that desk. Secretaries, I think they call them, when they have both a top and a bottom.

(*She holds up a sweater.*) Oh, here's a lovely sweater. Nile green. What do you mean—it's *not* my size. Why, I'm a perfect twelve. Wait, I'll show you! (*She places her purse on counter and struggles to get the sweater over her head. She works her arms vigorously and smiles nervously.*) Don't be silly, Flo. These things are always a little tight *before* they're washed. (*She finally gets the sweater over her head and attempts to pull it down.*) Help me, Flo! I—I can't seem to find the opening for my head and— There! Well, it's on, anyway. (*Quickly*) No, no, it's not too small. These things run in tight sizes, that's all!

And don't stand there, Flo. Help me get it off! (*She resumes her struggling until the sweater is off. She sighs heavily.*) Mercy, that was an ordeal! (*She holds sweater and waves her arm.*)

Oh, saleslady—please wait on me. Over here, please! Yes, this sweater. Nile green. (*She hesitates*) Oh, it's perfect—but there's something about Nile green. Now, if I could see the same thing—the *same* thing, mind you—in emerald green. (*Disappointed*) No—no emerald green? That is a shame. (*She waves her hand.*) Well, never mind. I'll just look around. Maybe I'll see one that looks like emerald green.

Of course I didn't buy it, Flo. You never buy the first thing you see at a sale. (*Brightly*) Now if I could find a perfectly plain black sweater, then I could have a monogram embroidered on it, and get one of those gold chokers with maybe some earrings to match— (*Breaks off and then speaks thoughtfully*) But if I were to buy that desk instead, I wouldn't have to worry about monograms and—

Call George? Gracious, no! Today's his monthly board meeting and I'm afraid he'd say "no" to anything I suggested. . . . Flo! Look! That woman—the one with the pink sweater—she's actually looking at my desk. (*Stamps her foot*) Some people are monopolistic. She just *can't* have it.

Now—now I think she's looking for a clerk. Yes, there he is—the sales clerk. Sure, I can tell . . . that funny little grin and the boutonniere and everything. And that woman is just beaming at him. She probably wants a discount and—and he's smiling at her too!

Oh, I wish sales clerks wouldn't smile like that. What? Oh, who cares about the sweaters? How—how could I think about them at a time like this? (*She brightens.*) She's walking away! Oh, Flo, such a narrow escape. (*She raises her hand and calls.*)

You . . . young man—yes, you with the boutonniere. I'd like to see that desk. Yes, I know it's called a secretary. Yes, it *is* lovely and I think it will do very nicely and—what? Sold! (*She points.*) That—that woman? She's going to leave a deposit and—*delivered tomorrow?*

(*Frostily*) Well, the very idea! Is it the policy of this store to sell merchandise under a prospective customer's nose? What—another desk? Of course not! It has to be a secretary, and it has to be mahogany and—never mind! (*She walks away.*)

Yes, Flo, that woman bought *my* desk and--and it's all George's fault. Now, if I had a husband like hers I wouldn't have to worry about the cost. (*She gestures at sweater counter.*)

Look—the sweater counter's completely sold out. There's not a thing left, except one of the shopper's shoes. Oh, she'll miss it when she gets home and—gracious! It's only a little after nine and we have the whole day left.

(*She stiffens and points.*) There's that horrible woman again. Pretend you don't see her. (*She turns her head and stares straight in the air.*) The nerve of some people! She probably came back to gloat about the desk and—why, I think she's looking for someone.

And there's the clerk—smug man! Still smiling. Honestly, I think it must be painted on. She's handing him something. I'd just love to hear what she's saying, Flo. Of course I'm not curious, but it might be something about the desk and—(*Excitedly*)—the clerk is putting the price tag *back!*

Hurry up, Flo! Oooops, pardon me, madame! (*She*

pushes right.) Oh, yoo-hoo! Young man—yes, you with the smile. Remember me? I asked you about the—er—secretary, and you said that someone had bought it, and . . . *what?*

Did you hear that, Flo? That woman isn't going to buy the desk, after all. Her husband thought that it was a trifle expensive, and — well, some men are like that. Fortunately, George isn't. George is the most generous husband—never questions any purchase I feel must be made. Flo, isn't it marvelous? My very own secretary desk. Expensive? Didn't I say $249.99? Well, yes, it is quite a lot but—Flo! Just look at this tag. It says $199.99. I must have read it wrong before. Isn't that wonderful! Why, just think, I'm saving George—let me see, $199.99 from $249.99—why that must be at least sixty dollars. Oh, won't George be pleased!

Now, where is that salesman? (*Waves and calls*) Oh, young man! Yes, right here. . . .Of course I'm going to buy it. You'll take a check, won't you? That's fine. I'll make it out right now. $199.99.

What? Four hundred and fifty dollars? My dear man, you must need glasses. Why, just look here—it says here right on the tag in plain numbers—$199.99. . . .Just for the *top*? And the bottom costs $249.99? Well, I think that's the most disgraceful way of marking things I've ever heard of. I suppose with a pair of shoes you mark each one $15.98 and sell the pair for—well, for whatever it is. . . . Why isn't it the same thing?. . . .Because the shoes can't be sold separately? Very well, then, young man, in that case I think I'll just take the glass top for $199.99.

No, Flo, of course I'm not crazy. For the time being,

we can put it on a card table, and then some day when George is feeling generous. . . . What's that, young man? You say you can't sell the two parts separately? But you just said the whole difference between this and a pair of shoes is that the shoes couldn't be sold separately —which, of course, implies that these two parts could be.

Mixed up? *I've* gotten *you* mixed up? Did you hear that, Flo? This young man has the nerve to tell me— *what?* Another sale? Where? You just heard someone say it was on the third floor? Typewriter tables? Let's go quickly.

What? Do we have a typewriter? No, of course not, but what does that matter? We can always pick up an old typewriter somewhere. Hurry Flo, please, before they're all gone. (*She grabs her friend's arm and hurries out.*)

THE END

5

Den Mother

> MRS. FRED HARLOWE, *a harried young mother, is speaking to her husband. The scene is the Harlowe home.*

Put that paint can away, Fred. No, no! You can't do a thing with the hall this afternoon. I know it's Saturday, but the paint job will have to wait. . . .

Now Fred, I *told* you those children were coming this afternoon. Oh, Fred, don't you ever listen when I tell you things? Tommy's cub scout troop. They'll be here in a few minutes. . . . Now, Fred, it's no use always asking why it has to be me. A mother should take an interest in her son's activities. A *father* should also take an interest—

Yes, at the meeting last Tuesday. Well, no, I didn't exactly volunteer. I merely raised my hand to ask a question and they elected me den mother of the month. Be-

29

sides, there are only four boys coming—five, counting our Tommy.

(*Calls*) Tommy! Tommy, come on down now, dear. Your little friends will be here any minute. . . . What? They're not your little friends? Yes, Tommy, I know they're cub scouts, but will you please come down this—

(*Nervously*) There's the doorbell now. Fred, please let them in. . . . (*Graciously*) Hello boys, come in. It's so nice to have you here, and— (*Staring*) five, six—seven, eight, nine—Fred, help! It's an avalanche.

Oh yes, Donald, how are you, dear? Oh—you brought your little brother? Well, dear, I don't know. If he promises to sit down and be a very good boy. Oh, and you brought your two cousins, Philip. They're visiting from Racine and your mother was sure I'd like to meet them. (*Nodding*) Yes, well, that was certainly very thoughtful of your mother. Yes indeed, I *do* understand. She had some shopping to do.

(*Turns left*) What's that, Fred? I'm not a den mother, I'm an unpaid baby sitter? Well, yes, dear, I'm afraid I — (*Screams*) Donald! Take your brother off the table. No, he certainly cannot play in that big bowl. That's for the punch. What punch? Why, the punch we're going to have later on when we have the refreshments. *Later on,* boys. *Later on!*

(*Calls frantically*) Tommy Harlowe, will you please come down here this *instant.* (*Turns left*) Honestly, Fred, here I go and do all this to stimulate Tommy's interest in scouting and—

Where did I put that den mother's manual? Oh, yes, here it is. (*Holds up book*) Now, boys—*boys!* Come along, boys. We're all going to form a semi-circle. Why not a full circle, Philip? Well—because the manual says a semi-circle.

Yes, Gregory, if you'll just wait, I'll tell you what we're going to do. Fred, dear—please hand me that rope—there on the mantel. Now boys, we're going to begin with a review of knot tying. Yes, that's right. (*Holds up rope*) You remember the timber hitch, don't you, boys? Yes, the timber hitch. (*Demonstrating with rope*) Now, we pass the end of the rope under and around the log. Where's the log? Well, Donald, we must use a little imagination. . . . Carry the end under and over the standing part. Twist the rope around its own part a few times and—

No, Philip! No—not around your cousin's neck. (*Screams*) Fred! Do something—get a knife, quick. The child is turning blue! (*Relaxes*) There—that's better. Now, we mustn't let ourselves get carried away like that, Philip. Oh—you confused it with the tourniquet lesson? Well yes, I suppose that could happen—but still, perhaps we'd better forget about knot tying today.

Let me see now. . . . (*Turns pages of manual*) Oh, you'd like to do nature studies next, Gregory? Well, isn't that sensible! Such a nice, quiet pastime. Oh, and you've brought some plant specimens. What a fine boy you are, Gregory. Such a help to den mothers.

(*Turns left*) What? What are you saying, Fred? Poison ivy? No, it couldn't be. And poison oak and poison sumac? Fred, get rid of them! Quickly! In the garbage pail. (*Sighs*) And now, Fred, will you *please* go upstairs and see what's happened to your son Tommy?

Now, Gregory, don't take on so. We do appreciate the

specimens but it just so happens that I'm allergic to poisonous things. Do I mean the plants? Of course I mean the plants.

Where's your brother, Donald? That's just it. He's *too* quiet. There's something very disquieting about a quiet child. What, Fred? *What?* The paint? All over the hall. (*Shakes head*) Oh, Fred. I *told* you to put it away. On my carpet? Well, don't just stand there, Fred. Get the turpentine! And get Tommy! You did? He's where? In his room reading a comic book, and you wouldn't mind joining him. . . .

Well, Donald, your mother shouldn't have let your brother wear his new shirt, then. If she thinks she has troubles, she should see my hall.

Oh, well, let's settle down again. More nature life. Well, yes, it is quieter . . . it's very interesting, too. Now, Gregory, perhaps you'd like to start the discussion since you seem to be the little naturalist of the group . . . You did *what?* A snake? (*Looking around in panic*) Where? Fred! Fred, come here quickly. No, I know you can't be in ten places at once, but there's a snake in here. What, Gregory? It slipped right out of your hand . . . and you saw it slither under the chair? Ohhh—you've got it, Philip? Good. Well, take it right outside. Yes, Gregory, I know it's your snake, but we must give the snake its freedom. You wouldn't want to think of that nice little snake all cooped up in the house.

My manual! (*Looks around*) Where's my manual? I don't know what I'd do without it. Oh, you don't think I'm doing so well *with* it, Fred? Well, I'd like to see you do very much better.

32

(*Picks up manual*) Oh, here's the manual. (*Turns pages*) Oh, yes—here's something nice. Fire by friction. (*Turns left*) Oh, Fred, of course it's perfectly safe. (*Hand cupped over mouth*) It never works. Tommy and I tried it outside for two hours the other day, and we didn't even get a spark. This will keep them quiet for hours.

What, Donald? Of course matches are easier, but after all, we're cub scouts. Suppose we didn't have any matches? A pocket lighter? Well, all right, Donald, if you don't want to be primitive, we'll let someone else have the flints. Who? Your little brother? Well, I hardly think he's quite old enough—oh, very well, if he'd like to try. At least it will keep him out of trouble for a few minutes.

Fred, will you bring in that plate of sandwiches—and the cookies—and the punch in the refrigerator? That's right—good. Now, boys, it's time for refreshments and —oh, there you are, Tommy! How nice you were able to tear yourself away from your comic book. And at such a suitable moment, too. Boys, here is your host—

Fred! I smell smoke! What? Your brother, Donald? He's set fire to the table leg—with the flints! Fred, throw some punch on the table leg. Yes, Donald, it *was* wrong to say he was too young. No, I certainly did not realize how smart he was. . . .

Now boys, come along and have some sand—gone? The sandwiches are *gone*? And the cookies—and the punch! Fred, did you ever see anything like it? The way they devoured that food. . . . Oh, your mother didn't have time to fix lunch? You haven't eaten all day, Philip—and your cousins haven't, either? My, your dear mother's had an enjoyable day.

And I thought the refreshments would take up far more time than that! I really don't know what to do next. . . . I don't mind the boys being active. It's the maddening little lulls that worry me. Thank heavens, the paint is in the cellar. What's left of it, anyway. . . .

Yes, Donald, you may take your brother. The first door to the left. Well, that's *two* less for a little while. Now, if we can demonstrate some simple little signals, that'll keep us out of trouble.

First we raise the semaphores—so. (*Demonstrates*) Now, we bring our left hand back, ever so swiftly, and—oh, Fred! Well, how did I know you were standing behind me? Here—sit down. It's just a little red, I think. Don't take on so. The cub scouts are watching.

Oh no, they're not. You're right, Fred—Donald and his little brother—*What?* The tub is flooded? Oh, you stopped up the drain with the towel, Donald? Quick, Fred, get a mop or a pail or something. I don't care if your brother likes Niagara Falls or not, Donald. . . .Take your shoes off, Fred. Roll up your pants. I'd better get back to the other demons—er—the other scouts.

Oh, you'd all like to play outdoors? Well, I don't know. We've always been friendly with our neighbors but—yes, at this point, I'll try anything!

Who's screaming outside? Mrs. Thompson? She—she found Gregory's snake? Poor woman! Well, you should have put it someplace else. Don't worry, I think they've revived her. She'll never forgive me. Never.

Now, boys, as I was saying—boys! Boys! Where have they gone, Fred? Out the front door—*all* of them? I—I can't let them run around the neighborhood. What will their mothers think? What will the neighbors think?

Quick—help me round them up! Yes, there's one behind the sofa. Philip's cousin. Get a good hold on his collar. And there's someone out in the azalea bush. Well, it used to be an azalea bush. I know—trampled to dust!

Boys! Boys! Come back this instant! (*She exits, wildly waving her arms.*)

THE END

6

The Super-Duper Market

> MRS. HARVEY SCHWEBEL, *a middle-aged housewife, enters, pushing a wire shopping cart. The scene is a supermarket on Saturday morning.*

Yes, Harvey, I know we went shopping Thursday night and I told you I'd bought enough for a week, but even so, there are bound to be a few little things one never remembers until Saturday morning. . . . Oh, you want to get to your golf game? All right. Don't worry. I just need a box of salt, and maybe a head of lettuce, and some eggs, granola, organically grown vegetables—there's our health to consider, you know—and there was something else. . . . I told you, Harvey, we won't be a minute.

(She looks around.) Now, let's see—where is the salt? *(Annoyed)* No, Harvey, it's really not in the least confusing if you just know in advance what you've come to buy and then head straight for the right aisle.

Oh, dear this can't be the aisle. (*Points to sign*) Records, flashlights, tooth paste, nylons, stuffed animals, charcoal, dog collars, clothesline—oh, good! I've been meaning to get some. Clothesline is the hardest thing to remember.

Oh—and look, there's that new low-calorie whipped cream we saw advertised on television. Let's try it. (*Holds up can*) The man on TV said you just turn the cap like this and—oh, goodness gracious, Harvey! I'm sorry. Did I ruin your shirt? Here, take my handkerchief, dear. I didn't realize. . . .

Oh, Harvey—here's just what we need—plastic playing cards, and on sale. The Atchesons are coming next week, and we'll simply have to play cards. There's nothing else to do with people like the Atchesons—except eat. And he has the appetite of an elephant. Come along, Harvey, we'd better get some cold cuts, party rye, slim-eze cream cheese, and crackers and peanuts right away. . . . Harvey, it will take only a minute and it will save me another trip next—

Oops! Oh, I *beg* your pardon. What's that? Well, I assure you I *was* looking where I was going. (*Pulls at cart*) Oh, dear, our carts are stuck together. . . . I assure you, sir, it was *not* my fault. Harvey, do something!

(*Looks in other cart*) Oh my, just look at those nice little cans of sardines they have in their cart. And those lovely chops, much leaner than the ones I saw in the case. . . . Excuse me. Where did you find those chops? . . . You had them cut to order? They've never done that for me! Well, maybe next time. Oh, and yogurt. I always forget about yogurt. Harvey, would you please go pick up a few containers of yogurt? I can untangle the carts.

(*She tugs at cart.*) Now—now sir, I think just one little

tug. . . . oops! Oh, I'm so sorry. . . . Well, how could I help it? You were pulling, too. And it won't hurt your potatoes to be all over the floor. You'll have to wash them anyway. And besides, you ran into me first. . . .

(*She turns.*) Oh good, Harvey. You found the yogurt. . . . What's that, dear? You hate yogurt? But it's so good for you—and 97% fat free, too. . . . All right, Harvey. All right. Let's not stand here arguing. Go get the sardines now and meet me at cold cuts.

What? What crowd? Oh, yes. They must be giving free samples of something. Honestly, the way people will stand in line to wait for anything free! . . . Come on, Harvey, push through. . . . There's an opening. (*She elbows her way forward.*) Free sauerkraut juice? Yes, miss, we'd love to try some. (*Takes cup and drinks*) It's delicious. Isn't it good, Harvey? (*Hisses at him*) Stop making such a terrible face! The demonstrator is looking at you. (*Smiles and nods*) Yes, miss, we'll take two cans— three—make it four. (*Puts cans in cart*) I believe sauerkraut juice is supposed to be very *good* for you. Full of vitamin C, I think, and if we mix it with tomato juice, we won't taste it at all. Honestly, Harvey, there's just too much to do these days. . . .

I've heard all about how well your mother managed a house. Things were different in those days. They didn't have all the modern conveniences. . . . What? . . . Well, something is always breaking down and then I have to wait around the house all day for the repairman to show up. . . . Oh, do hurry, Harvey! You were the one who was so anxious to get to the golf course.

Push our cart into that check-out line there. The second one. The one with nobody in it. What luck! No one ahead of us. . . . What's that, Harvey? No one checking people out, either? But there must be. They haven't put up that little barrier. . . . What miss? Your cash register is jammed? Another line? Oh, dear.

Harvey, quick! Slip in there! . . . No, of course you didn't sneak in in front of some nice, unsuspecting woman. Believe me, there is no such thing as a nice, unsuspecting woman in a supermarket.

Come on, let's unload the cart before anyone tries to push ahead of us. And this line has a bagger—you know, someone who puts the things into the bags. (*Starts taking things out of cart*) No, no, miss. Those are our things. They don't go with that order. They go with *our* order—oh, I beg your pardon, sir. Yes, of course I know it's possible for two people to buy clothesline and baked beans, but—yes, I do see that dividing stick. And please put out that cigar!

(*Shrugs eloquently at Harvey*) Such people! Oh, dear, now the bagger's gone to the next aisle—just when it's time to pack our things. Really! Do you have the money, Harvey? She's starting on our order now, and it takes them only a second. Then we'll be out of here. . . .

How much? $26.58. Imagine it, Harvey—$26.58. For nothing. . . .That's right, young man. Just put the bags in the cart. . . . Now, Harvey, that wasn't bad, was it? Even you must admit it didn't take long. I told you it wouldn't. I told you we needed only a box of—

Harvey! We forgot it! We forgot the salt! (*She pushes cart offstage.*)

THE END

7

First Day at School

> Miss Maltby, *a competent young woman,*
> *stands at a desk. She surveys the empty class-*
> *room with confidence, and then turns to*
> *speak to another person. The scene is the*
> *Fairview School Kindergarten on Opening*
> *Day.*

It was nice of you to come over this morning, Miss
Finger. Yes, I know you taught this kindergarten class for
thirty-five years before you retired. I may seem young to
you, but I assure you, Miss Finger, I am well trained for
this work. You see, I was a student of Professor Pickle's.
Who is Professor Pickle? Why Miss Finger, surely you
must have heard of him. He's the leading expert on group
psychology . . . an authority on all the modern child-
oriented research methods. Yes, indeed I have. I've planned

the entire day according to his techniques. You see, Miss Finger, teaching is a science.

The bell? Oh, good! Here they come! It's exciting to be starting your very first day! But there are so many of them. Droves and droves. The principal told me a very small class. And here come the mothers, too. Well, Professor Pickle always said that mothers must be firmly dealt with.

Now, children, take your places, please. I am Miss Maltby, your new kindergarten teacher. Oh yes, Mrs. Prentice, I'm very glad to meet you. And this is your little Gwendolyn? She's very talented? Well, don't worry, Mrs. Prentice—she'll be in good hands. I always encourage creative expression. Take your seat, Gwendolyn . . . take your *seat,* dear.

What did you say, Miss Finger? That dreadful child stuck out her tongue at me? Now, now, she's not a dreadful child at all. She's merely suffering from a slight behavioral block . . . obviously the result of over-permissive parents. But never fear. She'll be a different child after a term of applied psychology.

(*Calls*) Gwendolyn, I said take your seat, and I mean take your seat. Little boy . . . yes, you over there. What's your name? Alfred? Well, Alfred, we do not throw clay. Clay is used to develop your creative instincts, but throwing is not (*Ducks*) creative . . . What? Oh, you're Alfred's mother? How do you do . . . yes, I'm sure Alfred is a gifted child . . . yes, yes, of course I'm proud to have him in my class.

(*To Miss Finger*) What bedlam! I wonder if Professor Pickle ever met such children. The parents don't teach the children anything for five years, and then I'm expected to work miracles the first morning. If only all these mothers would go out. They keep looking at me as if I were going to infect their children with some horrible disease.

Well, I might as well try to get started. (*Claps her hands*) Attention, everyone. Attention, children. Now, first, I'd like to introduce myself. I'm Miss Maltby. M-A-L-T-B-Y. . . . I beg your pardon? No, Mrs. Greenfield, I'm not related to the Boston Maltbys. Oh, they're friends of your sister-in-law? Well, isn't that nice. But right now—heavens, Miss Finger, how can I ever create an effective relationship with these children if their parents keep interrupting? If I don't establish a group orientation right at the start—what? What *is* group orientation? Why, Miss Finger, group orientation means—well, I suppose in *your* terms it means getting acquainted.

Now, mothers, class will be dismissed at eleven forty-five and—Gwendolyn, we do not kick when we want attention. . . . Yes, Mrs. Prentice, I will remember she's very sensitive. Yes, *and* talented. (*To Miss Finger*) Obviously an aggressive child with hostile tendencies . . . a definite reaction formation.

No! No, little boy, we must not pull that little girl's hair. Here—take these blocks. No, *not* to throw at her—to build something, something imaginative. . . . Oh dear, where is my schedule? I must get started. I haven't accomplished a thing so far. (*Claps her hands*) Now children, I'd like you to call out your names and—no, *no!* (*She covers her ears.*) Not all at once. One at a time. I'll point to each one of you with this ruler and . . . what's that, little boy? Am I going to hit you with a ruler? Mercy, no.

Wherever did you get an idea like that? I'm just going to point to each one of you in turn.

Yes, little girl? (*She bends solicitously.*) Oh. Yes, you'll find it right out in the hall. Yes, you may go. But come right back. Oh dear, Miss Finger, I just hope she won't get lost. But if I stop every time for *that*, why, I'll never get anything done.

What's that? I'm not getting anything done as it is, you say? Well, I shall, never fear, as soon as I— Oh! Oh dear me, what's that? Little boy! Come out from under my desk this instant. No, no, Miss Finger, he is *not* shy. He is merely inner-directed. He must learn to identify with the group. Now, little boy, go over and stand with the other children . . . over there. Now children, get in line. Yes, that's right . . . form a line, everyone.

Oh, good. At last I have them all together in a group. Now I can re-direct their energies. Yes, a brisk march should do it. Then maybe the mothers will be ready to go home—once they see how nicely their precious darlings respond.

(*Loudly*) All right, children, when I give the signal we're going to have a little march. All around the classroom—won't that be fun? It won't be fun? (*Very brightly*) Oh yes, I'm sure it will be. Let's start now. One—two— three . . . (*Claps hands*) *March!* Yes, that's right. (*She marks time in place.*) Left, right, left, right. Now—you, the leader, turn. *Turn.* To the *rear* of the classroom. No, no, not forward. Go back! Go *back*, I say. Good gracious, Miss Finger, they're heading for the door! (*She runs to the door and stands, braced, arms outstretched.*) Back to

43

your seats. (*Frantically*) Back to your seats! Back! Back! (*Sighs in relief*) Goodness, that was a close one.

Well children, it's time for your mothers to leave now. No, no—Gwendolyn, don't tear Mother's dress that way. Oh, gracious, Mrs. Prentice, I hope you can repair the hem. (*Shouting*) Gwendolyn, don't scream so. Yes, indeed, Mrs. Prentice, she *is* a very articulate child. Yes, that's right . . . eleven forty-five. I'll be looking for you then. (*She clears her throat and takes a deep breath.*)

Now children, I'd like you to form *two* lines. That was the whole trouble before. I forgot to have them form *two* lines. Professor Pickle has always emphasized the importance of giving a child freedom of choice. *Limited* choice. No, no, children, don't start marching again. I didn't say you should march. And I said two lines.

Alfred, I told you not to throw that clay. And you, little boy, I said . . . and Gwendolyn, you *must not* kick that nice little girl—what? You have to go outside again? No, no, don't march! (*She folds her arms, clenches her teeth.*) I will not lose my temper. I will not lose my temper. (*Shouts*) I will not lose my temper! (*Bangs on desk*)

Children, for three years I have been a student of Professor Pickle. I have mastered his theories, his techniques, and his methods—and now I'd like to tell you something. If this class doesn't come to order immediately, (*Enunciates clearly*) I'm going to bash in your little heads!

THE END

8

The Driving Lesson

> EMMA CARLSON, *a young wife who is new to driving, sits perched behind the steering wheel. The scene is the front seat of an automobile.*

Come along, Godfrey. I've been ready for hours. (*She points to the seat beside her.*) There! For goodness' sake, Godfrey, don't grip the door handle like that! Gracious, one would think this was my first lesson. . . . Yes, of course I know where everything is, and what else is there to know? . . . Of course I'm relaxed. Why, when I see the idiots that can drive cars. . . . (*She settles in her seat and touches the knobs on the dashboard.*)

Let's see. What is it I do first? The key? Heavens, I knew I'd forget something. . . . Well, I think Joanne took it to school because her friend Caroline has the measles and—of course I'm making sense. You simply don't understand. Caroline has the measles—the German kind—and Joanne had to get some books out of the locker for her. Well, Joanne put Caroline's key on the chain with *our* car key. Really, Godfrey, you always make me go into such detail.

Oh, you have *your* key! Well, then, why make such a fuss? One little key is as good as another. (*She takes the key and inserts it delicately into the ignition. She frowns.*)

Godfrey—nothing happened. . . . Oh, the gas? Yes, to be sure. Well, I know you have to step on the gas—*so!* (*She jumps.*) Oh, I'm sorry, Godfrey—but please keep your feet where they belong.

(*She smiles and waves cordially.*) Good morning, Mrs. Alexander. . . . My first lesson? Oh, mercy, no. It's just that Godfrey doesn't trust those driving school people and insists on seeing for himself exactly how well I can drive before he even lets me venture around the block alone in the car. You know how men are, Mrs. Alexander. Always so fussy. . . .

(*She turns right.*) What, dear? Yes, I know you don't have all day. (*Hisses*) Must you be so *rude* to that sweet Mrs. Alexander? All right, Godfrey, have it your own way. She is not sweet. . . .

Well, it's not my fault that the car doesn't start. . . . What? The motor's cold? I—I should choke it a little? (*She shrugs.*) Anything you say, Godfrey, but it sounds terribly violent to me. (*Quickly, she grabs the steering shaft and begins to shake it. Then she stops.*) Oh—that little gimmick over there? Well, why didn't you say so? (*She pulls out the choke.*)

And still nothing happens! Why, some people merely get into their cars and shoot off—like *that*. (*She snaps*

46

fingers.) Well, it could be the fault of this car. After all, the thing is almost a relic and now that I'll be driving to town and to the bridge club and everywhere—well, a new car would be nice.

Step on the clutch? Now, let's see, which one *is* the clutch? (*She jerks violently*.) Oh, that was the gas? Yes, the brake pedal—I understand. And now a little gas and shift to first and release the clutch and. . . . I know, Godfrey. I know. I did it perfectly with the driving school man, but you get me all confused. (*She sniffs the air*.)

Godfrey, I think we've sprung a leak. Why, I can smell the gasoline and—yes, yes! I strangled—er—choked the car and—no. I—I left the handle like *that* and—flooded? Well, don't look at me like that. I can't help it if the gas flooded the motor. And stop muttering! Gracious, it's a warm day. Why, the old motor should dry out in no time at all!

Release the clutch? All right. (*She quickly lifts her foot off the pedal, and then shakes violently. She glances right and speaks sarcastically*.) Well, you told me to release it. I can't help it if the thing didn't hold. . . . Oh, gently? Now you tell me! (*She lifts her foot very slowly, and then looks right tearfully*.) Now the motor's stopped again. Well, perhaps I should choke it. . . . And you don't have to bark like that, Godfrey.

A little gas? There! Oh, good, we're finally moving. What? Shift into second, you say? What for? We have plenty of time. Why can't I keep going this way for a while? . . . Oh, all right, dear, but I do think you're being too particular. Just so long as the car goes forward. . . .

Godfrey! It's *not* going forward. We're backing up. Godfrey, *do something.* (*She stops with a jolt.*) Oh, dear. And it's all your fault. If you'd only let me go along the way I was going. . . . What? Oh, I'm sure they can fix the garage door.

(*She begins to giggle.*) You know, Godfrey, I think you have a little bump on your head. (*The more she looks at him, the more she laughs.*) It's getting bigger, Godfrey. We can fix it with ice. (*With an effort, she stops laughing.*) All right, dear, I know it's not funny.

Now, let's get started again. Oh, isn't that fine—we're off. First—and now I shift into second . . . you see how nicely I've learned, Godfrey. I might even try to get into third—Godfrey! That fence! It's in my way. (*Swerves*) Oh, my—that was a close one. But didn't I handle it nicely? What? There are two slats from the fence on the street? Oh well, never mind, we'll pick them up on the way home.

Yes, of course I'm paying attention. How else do you think this car would be moving so nicely if I weren't. . . . Oh dear, Godfrey, that light down there. The traffic light! It's going to change color, just when I was doing so— what? The brake. Now let's see, which one is the—oh. (*Lunges forward*) Yes, that certainly *was* a rough one. But I don't see how it can be my fault. The brakes are just too tight, Godfrey, and you'll have to get them fixed. . . . Oh, all right, Godfrey, we'll put ice on *both* bumps when we get home.

If we get home, you say. Why, I don't see how you can talk that way. Do you expect me to go right through a red light? It isn't red any more? Oh, my, so it isn't. Godfrey, why doesn't the car go? Stalled? And I suppose you're going to say that's my fault, too.

Why—why are all those people honking their horns? Well, they'll just have to wait until I get this thing started. (*She recites softly.*) Starter—first—gas—clutch—gas. Oh, Godfrey. The light is *red* again! They certainly don't give a person much time.

No, no—you may not take the wheel. I'm going to learn to drive this thing if it takes all day. And I don't care whether they're impatient or not. After all, I'm only a beginner and—now, that nice policeman over there understands. (*She gestures.*) Why, he's smiling at me.

Godfrey, that is *not* a sneer. And—and he's walking over. Well, he probably wants to give me some advice or something. (*She smiles cordially.*)

Good morning, Officer. Lovely day. Yes, I *am* learning to drive. That is, I've already learned, but my husband is just giving me a little tiny bit of extra practice. I'm going to get my license in a few days. . . . What, Officer? (*She nudges her husband and whispers.*) Godfrey, do as the Officer tells you. He wants to see your driver's license. Well, of course it's in your pants pocket—oh, your *other* pants? (*She turns and smiles weakly.*) There seems to be a slight misunderstanding, Officer. My husband forgot his license. . . .

(*Her smile fades.*) Over to the curb? Yes, Officer. (*Hisses to her husband*) What curb? It's all full of cars. . . . That tiny little space? Big enough for a moving van, you say? Well, it most certainly is not, Godfrey. And I don't know

49

how to park. After all, I've had only two lessons and I think it's mean of you to expect me to master a complicated thing like parking.

Oh, the policeman looks terribly angry. . . . How does he expect me to pull over to the curb when he's standing right there? Oh! I didn't mean to lean against the horn! I just wanted to warn him. (*Grimly*) Very well, then. Here we go. (*Calls*) I'm coming, Officer. I'm coming. . . . (*Screams*) Officer, look out. Jump, Officer! Jump!

THE END

9

Model Plane

⌘

GEORGE FELLERS *enters right and nods enthusiastically. He carries a scale model, gas-motor airplane. The scene is an open field.*

Yes, sir, Frank. There's nothing like getting out in the great outdoors for a healthy afternoon's sport with your son. I'm glad you could come along with Jimmy and me. (*He turns.*) Come on, Jimmy—let's get started. After all, we're going to fly this model plane together and—what? You'd rather stay home and play baseball with the boys? Get that, Frank? (*He turns again.*) Well, let me tell you something, Jimmy. That guy at the P.T.A. said every father should be a friend to his son, and I'm going to be *your* friend—see!

(*He points at plane.*) Yes, Frank, it's a pretty good plane, if I say so myself. Took me three weeks to build it. Oh, I

51

read all the books in the business. *Aeronautics . . . Wind Directions . . . Flying Techniques.* Well, if a fellow is going to have a hobby, he should know what he's doing. Not that it's my hobby, mind you. Oh, no! Jimmy's going to run the whole show. He just loves these flying jobs and— Now, Jimmy, you can join the Navy when you grow up. Right now, you're going to go all out for the Air Force.

That's right, Frank. It's a gas motor job. (*He nods.*) Fifty dollars. (*Shrugs*) Aw, it's only money. It's for Jimmy's own good and a father must help to shape his boy's future. That's why I chose a suitable hobby—for the boy, I mean.

(*He moistens a finger and holds it up.*) North by northeast—or is it northwest? Oh well, it's a *good* wind, whatever way it blows. (*He adjusts wings.*) Now, when I bring up the struts, we'll be all set. Be careful with that control box, Frank. When the plane's in the air, I'll take over the remote controls. (*Happily*) Brother, you've never seen anything like it. No, I haven't flown it yet, but the man at the hobby shop said that it was child's play and—

No, you can't carry the plane, Jimmy. Yes, you'll have plenty of time to take over—later. Right now, it's man's work. Very technical, you know. (*He turns impatiently.*)

All right, Frank—so it *is* the boy's hobby. He *still* has to learn to appreciate values first. And it's *my* fifty bucks! (*He raises his arms and prepares to release the plane.*)

Now, here it goes and— (*He heaves plane into the air.*) Quick, Frank, give me the control box. (*He takes box and adjusts dial.*) First, we must find the ascension indicator and— (*He looks into air*)—and *where's the plane?*

What? It landed over there—by that pile of rocks? But— but I can't understand it. (*Points at rocks*) It's not supposed to be over there. (*Points into air*) It's supposed to be *up* there! (*He adjusts control box.*)

Step back, Jim. Can't you see that I'm busy? All right, you can get the plane, but don't drop it. It's a fragile thing and I don't want it broken.

Oh, oh! Look at those two kids out there, Frank. They're going to try to fly their plane. Well, their father should be out there. That's what I've been talking about. No interest, no supervision. Poor kids. They're not facing the right wind direction and—*there it goes!* (*His eyes follow the plane's flight.*)

Yes, I'll admit it's a good take-off, but it's a big job for a kid. (*He watches the plane's gyrations.*) Loop-the-loop . . . nose dive . . . yes, it's a good plane, all right. (*He shrugs.*) Well, I guess that's what they call beginner's luck. (*He calls.*) Hurry up with that plane, Jimmy. (*To Frank*) I'll teach those kids how to fly a plane! (*He takes the plane from his son.*)

I guess I'd better give the plane a running start. Yeah, the wind's died down. I'll take off with it and—*here goes!* (*He runs around the stage holding the plane above his head.*) What? What are you saying, Frank? Watch—watch out for the gully? What gully? (*He trips and falls.*) Never mind, Frank. I know which gully you mean. (*Gets up, looks around*) The plane! Where's the plane? By the rocks again? Well, I didn't land on it, anyway. (*He waves finger.*) And let that be a lesson to you, Jimmy. Always watch out for gullies—and things!

Oh, I think Mom will be able to stitch your pants, Jimmy. (*Rubs back*) I—I wish she could do something for this cramp in my back!

You'd like to try the plane, Jimmy? How many times must I tell you about the technical work? Yes, I'll let you have the control box when the plane's in the air. (*Between clenched teeth*) If it ever gets there!

Why should I let him try it, Frank? He doesn't know anything about flying. Yes, of course I see those kids over there. Yes, I know their plane is still in the air. (*Impatiently*) They've probably been flying these things for years. What's the matter, Frank—are you trying to rub it in? Well, I'll show you.

(*He sends plane aloft with a mighty heave.*) There it goes! Right in the old updraft. (*He picks up control box.*) Now, I set this lever and turn on the switch and— Oooooowwwww! (*He dances around stage.*) Get a doctor! Call the ambulance! I—I've been electrocuted! (*Breathlessly*) Yes, yes, it must have been a short circuit. What? I—I touched an exposed wire? Well, an exposed wire has no right being there!

Yes, Jimmy, get the plane again. Yes, by the rocks. You know, Frank, the plane always manages to land in the *same* place. That's something, at least.

And, Jimmy, those clouds don't look too good. It's going to rain and I don't want the plane getting wet and— No, Jimmy, you may *not* go home and play baseball. Can't you get it into your head—this is *your* hobby. I'm doing this all for *you*. . . . No, it's not going to rain. I know I just said so, but how could I know the sun was going to come right back out again?

Now, let's get organized. As long as you're here, Frank, I can use your help. If you'd like to run with the plane while I take the control box—no, no, I'm not tired. Heck, I broke the record for the hundred-yard dash at high school—and it isn't *that* long ago—but I don't want you to feel we're leaving you out of things. O. K., start running. The wind direction? Oh, run in any old direction. I don't care. (*He watches Frank and claps his hands excitedly.*)

You got it, boy, you got it! It's going up! (*He turns.*) Watch out, you kids. Be careful of your plane. (*Proudly*) My plane is in the air!

Up . . . up . . . up . . . now, watch this loop-the-loop! Oh, I'll show them, all right. There's the first turn in the loop and—it's heading straight for the road! Wave those cars back—do something! It's going to crash, right into that car! (*He runs ahead.*)

Hey, that's my plane! Well, why were you driving on that side and—er—hello, officers! Er—er—yes, it's my plane, in a way. My boy Jimmy, here, is crazy about flying and—(*Quickly*) Here, Jimmy, take *your* control box. (*He thrusts box at Jimmy.*) A little accident! Yes, it certainly made quite a scrape in the car paint. (*Hopefully*) Are you sure that it wasn't scraped before the—oh, you are? (*He grins sheepishly.*) Now, if you'll send me a bill for the damage and—oh, no, it won't happen again. It's a new plane and we'll have the bugs worked out. Yes, thank you! (*Sternly*) Jimmy, take your plane! (*Politely*) Goodbye, officers!

Can you beat that, Frank? Fifty million motorists and that foolish plane had to scrape a policeman's car! It's not our day, Jimmy. It's not our day. (*He shakes head.*)

No, Jimmy, we should be heading for home. I'm sure it's going to rain, and I don't care if those kids *are* still flying their plane. What are they trying to do—establish an endurance record?

And keep out of this, Frank! It's my son's hobby and I

say it's too late. Oh, you'll run with the plane again? O. K., one more try!

Good boy! I don't know how you do it, but you always manage to get it up there. Yes, yes, there it goes. Gosh, I almost forgot the control box! (*He stoops and picks up control box. He watches the plane proudly.*)

Did you ever see anything like that? Why, it's like a little dot up there. (*He calls.*) How do you like that, kids? Look at my plane! Yes, that little speck. What? Too high? Why, don't be silly. I know how to build 'em, that's all. Hear that, Frank? The poor kids are burning. Trying to tell me the plane will be carried away in the updraft. Yep, their father should spend more time with them, all right. (*He adjusts dials on control box.*)

Well, now to bring it around for a perfect three-point landing. We'll turn this little gadget once and— (*He looks up.*) That's funny. The plane didn't turn around. Well, maybe the wrong button. Nope, that doesn't work, either. Keep watching that plane, Jimmy.

I—I can't see the plane, Frank. (*Trace of panic*) Why, it might land in Siberia for all I know. Yes, get the car, Frank. Quick! There—there's the plane. That little speck. Oh! Oh! It's gone again. It went that-a-way! (*He tosses control box on the ground and calls to boys.*)

There's a control box for you, kids. Naw, we won't need it. My boy is interested in the Navy. That's right, Jimmy, the Navy. We're going to build some clipper ships—the kind that sail and—Frank, get the car going and—*follow that plane!* (*He exits quickly.*)

THE END

10

Do or Diet

> MRS. MABEL THORNE, *a trim, efficient,*
> *middle-aged woman, strides briskly onstage.*
> *Downstage left there is a placard on an easel,*
> *which reads:* CALORIE COUNTERS.

Good morning, loyal members of the Calorie Counters.
First, let's begin by repeating our motto: Think thin! Live
thin! Be thin! Or, in the immortal words of our glorious
founder, Mrs. Ellen Broadbeam—once a towering two-
hundred-pound mass and now a trim one hundred and
twenty—DIETING IS MIND OVER PLATTER!

To begin our meeting, I wish to introduce Mrs. Morley
who joined our group last week. As you may remember,
Mrs. Morley weighed one hundred and seventy-five pounds
when she came to us. I immediately prescribed the Calorie
Counter Never-Fail Diet. (*Dramatically*) Now we shall
weigh Mrs. Morley and see the dramatic results. (*She beck-*

ons and pantomimes guiding MRS. MORLEY *to scale, then adjusting weights and balances, and peering at figures on scale. She steps back, aghast.*)

One hundred and eighty-two! Oh, no! Mrs. Morley, how could you? You've gained seven pounds. (*Stamps her foot*) How could you? You couldn't have followed the Calorie Counter special 1500-calorie diet. What? Now, really! I distinctly said 1500 calories a *day*. You thought I said 1500 calories a meal? Dreadful! Plus between-meal snacks? (*In despair*) Friends, that means that Mrs. Morley has eaten thirty thousand calories since our last meeting. (*Turning and gesturing wildly*) Naughty, naughty, Mrs. Morley! For shame! You'll have to be punished! You will live on safflower oil and carrot tops until our next meeting! (*Shaking her head sadly*) What some people won't do to deceive the Calorie Counters. But our scales never lie! (*Slight pause, then she clears her throat, smiles, looks briefly around.*)

Next, we'll weigh in Mrs. Fitzgerald. (*She beckons toward right, and pantomimes moving someone onto scale, adjusting weights and balances, etc.*) What's that, my dear? You've lost ten pounds? Marvelous, simply marvelous. (*Leans forward and peers intently at scale*) But you haven't lost an ounce, not a single ounce! Oh, your husband lost ten pounds on our diet? He's down to a hundred and forty? Poor man! (*Shrugs*) But a husband must be prepared to make any sacrifice if he wants a trim and attractive wife. (*Smiles, then frowns*)

I am sorry to report that one of our vigilant members saw a fellow Calorie Counter sneaking into the Village Sweet Shoppe before our meeting today. Shocking, absolutely shocking! (*Shakes finger at audience*) Don't look so innocent, Mr. Atherton! *You* know you were there! (*Tossing her head, angrily*) No, I will not accept any excuse, Mr. Atherton. . . .Oh, you were just buying a box of candy for your mother-in-law? (*Sarcastically*) Sure you were, and I suppose that's why there's a big smear of chocolate sauce on your chin—your third chin! (*Sighs, then smiling again*)

Now, on a happier note, I wish to report the splendid progress Mrs. Summers has made. You'll remember that when she joined us, she couldn't get her three-carat diamond ring on her finger to wear to her niece's wedding. Since she came here, she followed the Calorie Counters diet right down to the last calorie, did our special finger exercises, and now, she not only got it onto her finger, but she almost lost it down the drain when it slipped off. Isn't that wonderful news, ladies? Of course, she is still a two-hundred-pound mound, but she has the slimmest finger in the class. (*Brightly*) Mrs. Summers, we salute you—especially your slender finger!

And now for a vital part of our program . . . (*Takes paper from table*) the Calorie Counters list of suggested foods for the coming week. (*Reading*) We must concentrate on okra, sauerkraut, celery juice, soy bean patties, frankfurters, no longer than five and one-half inches. (*Looking up*) And have you all been weighing and measuring your food portions? (*Sarcastically*) From all appearances, several of you must have been using yardsticks. (*Resumes reading*) Now, back to our list . . . Gelatin powder, dried apples, guava . . . (*Looks up*) How should I know what guava is,

Mrs. Bell? If our founder recommends guava, we eat guava!

Now, don't these foods sound absolutely delicious? Can you imagine a tantalizing salad of okra and sauerkraut, with some celery juice—just a soupçon, you know—drizzled over it? Or a bowl of dried apples and guava, with a shake of gelatin powder—a mouth-watering delight, I'm sure you'll all agree. What's that, Mrs. Bell? You say your husband wouldn't like that diet? (*Smugly*) Well, he'll just love the new *you!*

Some of you have asked me if people with large frames should have more nourishment. (*Sighing*) Now, friends, let's get this cleared up right away. Not all of you *have* large frames. As you know, Calorie Counters does make allowances for the small-frame, medium-frame, and large-frame man or woman—(*Annoyed*) Mr. Atherton, you do not have a large frame. It's merely the surrounding territory that makes you look that way! And it is not all right for you to weigh one hundred and ninety. None of you must ever forget the motto of Calorie Counters: DIETING IS MIND OVER PLATTER!

As your local group leader, I am always seeking new methods of keeping you away from high-calorie foods which are our greatest enemy. Last week I introduced a knife and fork with small batteries attached. As the eater picks up these utensils, he or she suffers an electric charge, and thus remembers to stay away from forbidden foods. Mrs. Fleming, a charter member of Calorie Counters, offered to use these utensils for a week. We shall now hear her report. (*Looks around*) Mrs. Fleming, if you please. (*Pauses*) What, she's not here today? She's in the hospital? What's that? You say she used the knife and fork and lit up like a neon sign? Oh, dear. We'll have to send her a little present—nothing over one hundred and fifty calories, of course!

(*Pause*) And now, as is our weekly custom, I myself will weigh in. (*Looks at wall and points*) My chart indicates that I was one hundred and thirty last time. We'll now see what progress I've made on the Calorie Counters wonder diet—which I followed diligently, of course. (*Pantomimes stepping on scale, jiggling weights and balances. She smiles elatedly.*) One hundred and twenty-five! There, you see, friends? I've lost five more pounds, thanks to the scientific program of Calorie Counters—and the inspiration of its founder, Mrs. Broadbeam. (*Suddenly looks left*)

Young man, what are you doing here? What? You're from the Acme Scale Company, and our scale is due for its yearly accuracy test? (*Impatiently*) There's absolutely nothing wrong with our scale. (*Annoyed*) Oh, very well. Check the scale, and do it quickly so we can proceed with our meeting. (*To audience*) Male chauvinist! (*Taps her foot impatiently*)

As soon as you've verified the accuracy of our Never-Fail Scale, you may leave—what? It weights ten pounds light? That's impossible. You don't know what you're talking about—ten pounds light, indeed! (*Suddenly horrified*) Ten pounds light! That means that instead of losing five pounds, I actually gained five pounds! (*Melodramatically*)

I'm unworthy to be a leader for Calorie Counters. A five-pound gain—the shame of it! (*Starting off, then turning back*) But remember, friends—Think thin—live thin—be thin! (*Runs off*)

THE END

11

The Introduction

> MRS. M. OGLETHORPE ALLEN *is presiding at a meeting of the Tuesday Afternoon Literary Society. She taps her gavel delicately upon the table.*

Attention, ladies, attention. Members of the Tuesday Afternoon Literary Society, we are indeed grateful to have Miss Forsythia Terwilliger with us today. Miss Terwilliger, noted author and world traveler, has many exciting and wonderful things to tell us. Because of her extreme popularity, she must leave immediately after her lecture to keep an appointment in—in— (*She turns left.*) Where are you speaking tonight, dear? Oh, yes. Schenectady. Wonderful town. Marvin and I spent two weeks in Schenectady in 1979. Or was it 1980? Well, never mind. Therefore, we will dispense with the usual introduction. . . .

Oh, yes, Miss Terwilliger, you'll make the plane. First of all, I must review the minutes for our last meeting. As you know, our dear member, Mrs. Fensterwald, has been hospitalized and it was decided to send her a little gift. Oh, yes! I called her doctor and asked for a complete report. Nasty thing! The doctor, I mean. He was rather adamant, but when I told him that Mrs. Fensterwald was a fellow club woman and her welfare was dear to our hearts, he prepared a brief report. Mrs. Fensterwald is suffering from— (*Riffles papers on table*) Now, where did I put that report? I know I had it this morning. (*She drops several papers.*) Yes, I know, Miss Terwilliger. In a minute! (*She picks up paper.*)

Ah, here it is! (*Reading*) "She is suffering from a snapped rudder and must have the barnacles thoroughly scraped off." (*She looks up.*) Oh, dear, that can't be right! (*She smiles weakly.*) Of course! This is Marvin's report. He's a maritime engineer and this must be his findings for the salvage committee. Now, how did I get it? Poor Marvin! He must have taken the report about Mrs. Fensterwald. Oh, well. I'm sure the salvage committee will understand.

Please, Miss Terwilliger. I have not forgotten the introduction.

Ladies, in view of the time— (*She looks sourly at Miss Terwilliger.*) I think it is fitting and proper to introduce our guest speaker. (*She picks up a paper and reads.*) "Miss Terwilliger is a woman well versed in the arts." (*Dreamily*) Yes, the arts. And the Tuesday Afternoon Mothers simply adore the arts! The plays of Molière. I loved *Tartuffe*. There are some people who prefer *Le Misanthrope*. Of course, there are others who don't like Molière at all. He's too—too French, if you know what I mean.

But, oh, yes! Miss Terwilliger. (*Reads*) "A woman who has traveled extensively among the Russians, Italians, Serbs, Croatians—" (*Turns left*) Croatia? Is there such a country, my dear? Yes, of course. It's so difficult to identify countries today, when they change names so much. But we women love books about travel. It removes us from this everyday, humdrum world of ours. Of course, I enjoy a good novel occasionally. Pearl Buck. About China—and things. (*She shakes her head sadly.*) And the American novel. Really, ladies, do you think it will ever find itself? Ah, the days of Faith Baldwin and Fanny Hurst. Call me sentimental if you will, but I love those sweet stories with a good cry on every page. Why, when I finished a book, the pages were limp with my tears—positively limp. But it did me so much good. The hero reminded me a little of Marvin, although I could never quite understand why.

Please, Miss Terwilliger, don't be nervous. Just a moment. (*Low*) Don't tug at your pearls, my dear.

Ladies, I've run away with myself again. Naughty girl —but I do look forward to our little meetings. It's so difficult to discuss things at home with a husband. You know what I mean. You have husbands. (*Glances over audience*) Or most of you, anyway. That Marvin of mine! He never takes his nose out of those horrid murder mysteries. I really can't see it. They're always the same— filled with doddering old ladies and retired colonels and Long Island estates. When you've read one, you've read them all—that's what I tell him. Really, it's so difficult to improve a man's mind these days. (*Quickly*) Not that there's anything wrong with Marvin's mind. Oh, mercy, no! (*Worried*) Oh, dear. I hope he won't be too upset—about Mrs. Fensterwald's problems, I mean.

Five minutes, Miss Terwilliger? Oh, dear, don't worry about the train. It's always late—well, of course I'm not sure it will be late today but all right—I'll hurry along with the introduction. . . .

(*She reads.*) "Our guest speaker is well versed in matters of world economy—" (*Looks up*) That's an amazing thing. Really, I never could understand economy. All this talk about inflation, money market funds, IRA and Keogh plans, stocks, bonds—(*Throws up hands*) It's just overwhelming! All I know about money is, it's here one minute, and gone the next. And no matter what I do, my checkbook never balances! . . .Now, where was I? Oh, yes. World economy. (*Reads*) "Miss Terwilliger is a woman with a vast knowledge of political science. She has met world leaders." (*Looks up*) She has met congressmen, too. But I'll let her tell you about that. She's had so many experiences—and I know you'd rather hear it from the horse's mouth, as it were. (*She turns left.*) Oh, I didn't mean anything personal, Miss Terwilliger. This speech sounded so—so nice when I wrote it. Of course not! Yes, in a minute. (*She turns and reads.*)

"Her writing is always so lucid. I remember her clever little book about the people in Bali. So inspiring!" (*Looks up*) It discussed the native customs—and women—and things. I couldn't put the book down. Simply never. . . . (*She turns left.*)

What is that, Miss Terwilliger? You've never been to Bali? . . . Someone else wrote the book, you say? Well, it's a lovely country—or nation—or island—or whatever it is. Yes, you must visit it, I'm sure. (*She turns.*)

Gracious, ladies, I don't know how I could have made such a mistake. All Miss Terwilliger's books are in my library. If I'm not mistaken, they're next to George Bernard Shaw's.

(*Turning left*) Now, Miss Terwilliger, you seem to have broken your pearls. Never mind, my dear. The cleaning woman will get them. She comes in every Wednesday, you know. We'll send them to you, if you want them. Yes— yes, the introduction. (*Coldly*) I am fully aware of the time. (*She turns, slightly annoyed.*)

Because of Miss Terwilliger's schedule, we will dispense with the usual introduction. (*She studies audience.*) Yes, Mrs. Fullerton, you may have the floor. Oh, I'm so sorry. You must leave? Yes, your son mustn't miss his violin lesson. Of course, we understand. My sister's boy studies the violin, too. Such a well-pitched, sensitive little thing. The violin, of course. Yes, yes. Oh, Miss Terwilliger will understand.

(*She turns left*) Miss Terwilliger, please! You needn't tug at my sleeve to remind me! (*Low*) Such impatience!

(*She addresses audience.*) Gracious, I'm all in a dither. Did I mention Miss Terwilliger standing with George Bernard Shaw? Yes, yes! I am so proud of the library. It's all been done over—a complete renovation. Unfortunately, the new color scheme doesn't do too much for the book jackets—but, then, the jackets don't do too much for the color scheme. Eventually I'll have to buy all new books. But that's one thing I like about literature. It's so—so flexible!

(*She draws herself erect, smiles proudly.*) This is the thrilling moment, ladies! It is my great pleasure to introduce Miss Forsythia Terwilliger!

(*She turns left.*) Miss Terwilliger. . . . (*She frowns.*) Miss Terwilliger! (*She calls.*) Oh, Miss Terwilliger! (*She turns to audience.*) Why, I can't understand it. She's gone! Why, I never—

Can you imagine that, ladies? How rude! She just up and left. (*Snaps fingers*) Oh, I'm terribly sorry. We should have engaged that woman from Brockton who does things with ceramics. (*She nods righteously.*) Well, we must be more selective in the future. Gone! Hmph! That woman should see a doctor about her nerves. Definitely emotional! But, ladies, what else can one expect from a person who writes? (*She frowns distastefully and sits.*)

THE END

12

It's Magic

⋅⋅⋅✦⋅⋅⋅

> PROFESSOR HIGGINLOOPER, *a pompous in-*
> *dividual in a cape and top hat, enters. He*
> *waves a wand dramatically. He may speak*
> *with an accent, if desired. The scene is a*
> *high school stage. There is a table in the*
> *center.*

Good afternoon, pupils! My name is Professor Higgin-
looper. I have been invited here today to entertain you
with tricks of sleight-of-hand, legerdemain—well, it's magic
to you! Now, you must all concentrate. Yes, that's right.
You know what concentration is. It's the thing you're
supposed to be doing in Latin class while you're thinking
about the latest rock-'n'-roll record! (*He waves wand
dramatically.*)

Now, one of the pupils will act as my assistant. I chose
a young man shortly before the show, and he consented

to appear on the stage. Where is that young man? (*He points into audience.*) Ah, there you are! All right, son. First, I'd like you to get a coat from a member of the audience. Ah, good! You have one already. Now, will you please come up here? (*He gestures to stage apron*) And be careful! Oh, no! Here, I'll help you up! (*He reaches across apron and helps young man to feet.*)

(*He takes coat.*) Now, I will rip a button from this suit jacket and prepare to have it sewed on—magically! (*He tugs at jacket button.*) This button is certainly well sewed on and—oh, no! (*He displays coat.*) There seems to have been a little accident and—yes, the coat. Torn right down the middle! (*He addresses assistant.*)

But I told you to take the coat from the boy over *there!* (*He points to right of audience.*) What? You forgot? You got it from the teacher over *there?* (*He points to left of audience.*)

All right—now, for the *next* trick. (*He glares at the assistant.*) I hope you put the *right* hat on the table. (*He smiles uncomfortably.*) Well, that's better.

Now, ladies and gentlemen, I am going to use an ordinary hat for the next feat. I will smash an expensive wristwatch, mix it with flour, water, and eggs—and deposit the whole thing into the hat! Then, with a flick of my magic wand, I will restore the watch to its original condition. (*He holds up watch.*) You see this watch. Now, I take the hammer and hit the watch—so! (*He puts watch down on table and hits it vigorously with hammer.*) Now the watch goes into the hat. (*He puts watch into hat, then picks up cup of flour.*) I cover the watch with flour—so! (*He pours flour into hat.*) Now, the water. (*He picks up*

70

pitcher of water and pours it into hat.) Now, I break the eggs—and into the hat they go. (*He breaks eggs into hat. Then he sticks both hands into hat and stirs violently.*) Ah! What a nice sticky mess I have. (*He takes out his hands, wipes them off, picks up his wand and waves it dramatically.*) And now, you will see that— (*He stares at the hat in puzzlement. Then he whispers to his assistant.*)

Did you get this hat where I told you? What? . . . Yes, it was in my car outside and—a green car with a white top? . . . No, no! I own a white car with a green top! (*He looks at member of audience.*)

What's that, sir? Oh, you're the principal? And you own a green car with a white top? *Yo—your* hat? Hah! Hah! (*He laughs weakly and stares at hat.*) Yes, it is pretty messy, isn't it? You see, I own a trick hat and I thought—well, perhaps, you can have it cleaned. . . . Ha, ha! Pupils, your principal has a good sense of humor!

Now, I will mystify and astound you with this disappearing shirt trick. My assistant, here, will unbutton his cuffs and the neck button of his shirt. Then, with a simple manipulation, I will remove his shirt without taking off his coat. (*He whispers to assistant.*)

Are you ready for this one, boy? Well, did you put your shirt across your shoulders as I showed you? What do you mean . . . there wasn't time? But, the audience, they're waiting to see the trick. Well I can't help that. We'll have to hope for the best! (*He tugs violently at shirt, and then holds ears and grimaces. He whispers to assistant again.*) I told you not to put your arms through the shirtsleeves! (*He grins uncomfortably at the audience.*)

A slight miscalculation, folks. My assistant didn't follow

my instructions. (*He pauses as though someone is tugging at his coat. He addresses the assistant.*)

Well, I can't help it if your shirt is ruined and—I am *not* going to pay for the shirt! If you had done as I told you and—so what? Your father used to be light-heavyweight champion in college, and—*light heavyweight champion!* (*He pats assistant's head.*) Oh, yes, yes, little man! We'll make good for the shirt, all right! Yes, indeed. (*His forced smile freezes into a sullen mask as he addresses audience.*)

For my final offering of the program, I am going to place an egg in my mouth and make it disappear—before your very eyes! (*He picks up egg and turns to assistant.*) I told you to get a *small* egg. Why, this thing looks like a grapefruit. Oh, it was the only one left. (*He nods.*)

Well, it's too late to do anything about that now. (*He examines egg apprehensively and turns to assistant again.*) And what's the matter with you now? Why are you sniffling and coughing like that? Well, it's very distracting—you're ruining my act! Please be quiet!

(*He places the egg into his mouth. He picks up his wand and gestures dramatically. Suddenly, he swallows hard and clutches his throat. His cheeks are swollen and his eyes dance wildly. Frantically, he points to his mouth as he sinks to his knees. He grabs at his collar. Finally, he swallows, sighs, and rises to his feet.*)

(*Glaring at the assistant*) I—I told you not to *sneeze* like that! You startled me so I swallowed the egg. (*He shakes his head sadly.*) And that's the end of our demonstration, ladies and gentlemen. (*Turning to his assistant*)

Oh, young man, I want to thank you for your *valuable*

72

assistance! Yes, my act will never be the same again. (*He picks up the hat which contains the broken watch, water, eggs and flour.*) Your cold? Well, you should get right home and—put on a hat! Here—take *this* hat. Your principal doesn't want it back! (*He jams the hat on the assistant's head. He nods emphatically and exits.*)

THE END

13

The Fish Story

> MOLLY SINGLETON *enters, groping in the dark. She finally reaches the boat moored to the landing. The scene is a mountain lake in early morning.*

Tom—Tom, where are you? I can't see a thing. Ah, your hand. Now, just help me into the boat. . . . Really, I can't understand why you insist upon fishing before five o'clock in the morning. The fish might not even be awake yet.

I am *not* trying to be facetious. After all, this fishing vacation was your idea and—what? I could have stayed home? With the scrubbing and the washing and the cleaning—I am *not* raising my voice. Anyway, how do you expect the fish to hear me—way down there in the water?

This boat seems pretty flimsy to me. It's wobbling. Perhaps I should sit at the other end. (*She stands uneasily and prepares to walk to the rear of the boat.*) Be careful,

Tom, you're rocking the boat. Oops, my foot's caught! (*She falls heavily into the stern of the boat and rubs her ankle.*)

Well, at least you could ask if I'm all right. So what—the old reel went overboard. You have another one, anyway. You'd probably like me to fall overboard and—

Oh, all right! Now, let's see—did I remember everything? Sandwiches, coffee thermos, cake . . . What did you say, Tom? The bait? What! You put those disgusting little worms in my sandwich cooler? Oh, Tom, you didn't! I don't care whether they should be kept on ice or in the fire. I won't have them eating my peanut butter sandwich.

Ugh—squiggly little things! No wonder it's so easy to catch fish. If anything is silly enough to eat these things, it deserves to get caught. (*She sits for a moment in silence. Then she sighs heavily and begins to fidget.*)

Tom—it's so stupid just sitting here. Why not let me row for a while? Please, Tom—of course I know how. Just give me the oars. Well, it's not fair for you to do all the work. (*She giggles.*) I think it's going to be fun. . . . Why, there's nothing to it. All you do is lower the oars into the water and push—or is it pull?—well, it doesn't make any difference. The lake is so big that it doesn't matter where we land.

(*She begins to row.*) I wish someone would tell these mosquitoes about Daylight Saving Time. Honestly, they're coming in hordes and— (*She drops the oars and slaps her arms.*) Oops! I almost lost the oars. (*She picks up the oars and tugs hard.*)

I don't think we're getting anywhere at all. Why, we're still at the landing dock and—what's that rope for, Tom?

The anchor? Well, you could have pulled it up! I think you did that on purpose.

Yes, yes, I know the fishing laws. Heavens, I've heard nothing else for the past three months. The fish must be seven inches long and—oops! Tom, we've hit something! Are—are we going to sink? (*She suddenly leans over and smiles.*)

Oh, we're terribly sorry. I didn't see your boat. Oh, you were just pulling in a bite and it got away? Well, the fish must still be around, and I'm sure you'll find it again. Oh—since one o'clock this morning? Your first bite? (*Uneasily*) Well, smooth sailing—and all that. (*She continues to row with renewed vigor.*)

Well, I didn't see his boat, Tom. In all this big lake, did he have to be right there? (*She drops oar to indicate the position.*) Tom—the oar! I lost the oar! Here, I'll help you look for it. Now, don't lean over too far and— (*She shouts.*) Take your head out of the water, Tom! (*She helps him back to a sitting position.*)

Well, we'll just have to make do with one oar, I'm afraid. What's so funny about that, Tom? After all, it's just a question of tugging a little harder—like this— putting all your steam on one oar, making it do the work of two. (*She tugs strenuously on one oar.*)

We're going around in circles? But why should we be? Because we have only one oar. But that's the most ridiculous thing I ever heard of. Why should two oars make you go straight, and one oar make you go around in— oops. . . . Oh, Tom, I feel dizzy. Stop laughing this instant. Here we are, doomed to spend the rest of our lives on this nasty little lake going around in circles and all you do is sit there and laugh. What? Might as well fish? Very well, then. We'll fish. And perhaps the Coast Guard will rescue us, since you seem to be incapable of doing anything about it.

All right, sit there and pout. See if I care. But you could at least be a gentleman and offer to bait my hook. Of course I'm going to fish—but don't expect me to stab that poor little defenseless worm. (*She cringes as she watches him bait the hook.*) How do you know the worm doesn't feel it?

Oh, I know how to cast. I've been watching it on TV for years. (*She waves pole in a wide circular pattern and finally heaves the line.*)

What—who's that? Yes—that scream. It came from over there. (*Points right*) Oh, thank you, sir! Yes, it's my fish hook. It landed—*where?* Oh, gracious! Well, if you'll use a pillow or a rubber ring, I'm sure it will be better in a day or two.

Isn't he an old grouch, Tom? And did you hear the language he used? Why, the nerve of him! Well, it was an accident—and it's not my fault if our boat bumped into his a while ago. Yes, dear—I'll try to be more careful.

Well, that man is probably miles away by now. . . . (*She waves the pole and the line sails through the air.*) Now, wasn't that nice casting? You see—even you have to admit it.

What do I do now, Tom? Just sit here and—wait? Well, if this isn't the most boring. . . . Oh! Oh! (*Softly*) Tom . . . Tom. I think something's on the end of my line. I can feel it. (*She tugs at the line.*) Help me, Tom. I—I can't hold it . . . Reel it in? Yes, I know that, but I don't think anyone told the fish.

Quick, get the net. (*She reels. Finally, the fish is hauled into the bottom of the boat.*) Oh, keep it away from me! It looks positively savage—but then, I can't really blame it. . . .

Stop jumping around that way, Tom. You're going to upset the boat. (*She holds the fish up and clucks disapproval.*) Now, isn't that a shame? (*Sighs*) Well, that's my luck! (*She heaves the fish overboard.*)

What on earth is the matter with you, Tom? Screaming at me that way. . . . But of course I threw it back. Well, you wouldn't want me to get into trouble . . . Yes, yes, it was a whopper. But you told me a fish must be *seven* inches long and that thing was well over two feet! What? . . . Well, how did I know that's the whole point of fishing? I thought they had to be seven inches—no less— and no more. Those fishing laws should be more explicit.

All right, then—don't let me fish again. I'll just sit here and think sweet thoughts, about what a nice trip we're having and what a nice companionable husband you are, and—Tom! You're bobbing! I—I mean the line's bobbing. Yes, you have a strike. . . . Oh, it's a beauty. Wonderful . . . wonderful! Oh, darling, I'm so proud of you. (*She stands and almost upsets the boat. Quickly, she looks over the side.*) It's all right, Tom. I'll help you out of the water. . . . Don't worry—the fish is still in the bottom of the boat. (*She helps him into the boat and then sits.*)

We must get you back to shore and into some dry

clothes. Then you can tell the chef at the lodge about the fish and he'll—what do you mean, have it stuffed? Over our fireplace? . . . And look that creature in the eye every night before dinner—certainly not! If you're not going to eat it, you shouldn't have bothered to catch it. And—oh, Tom, look! Here comes that pesky man again. Yes, you know the one—he practically crashed into our boat. Yes, he kept my fishhook, too.

(*She stands authoritatively and calls*.) Yes? What do you want? Well, of course we are—not that it's any of *your* business! (*Turns*) Did you hear that, Tom? He wants to see our license. (*She turns again*.) Let me tell you something. We've been married for ten years and—

A fishing license? Well—er—I don't know. You—you *don't* have a license, Tom—to fish, I mean? (*She smiles foolishly*.) No—no fishing license. Don't let that worry you, though. No one ever bothers you about a license up here. Tom told me that. Oh, yes, I'm sure it's all right and—oh, Tom. He's the fishing warden!

A fine? Well, the very idea . . . He wants us to appear before the magistrate, Tom. . . . But you told me that you've been fishing here for years without a license and I only quoted— (*She turns*.)

You'll have to tow us back to shore. Yes, I lost an oar when you crashed into our boat and— (*She frowns and speaks coldly*.) I'd also like my fishhook back, if you don't mind! (*She nods righteously, sits and folds arms*.)

THE END

14

Kiddie Matinee

❧❧❧

> MRS. SALLY SMITHERS *enters and smiles apologetically. The scene is the Orpheum Theatre, late Saturday afternoon.*

No, I don't want a ticket, young lady. I'm only here to call for my son, Albert. . . . Yes, at one today. Five hours ago. . . . Oh, I'm sure he's still inside. Yes, the kiddie matinee. . . . Yes, I know where he usually sits. That is, when he does sit. He likes to walk around—the soda fountain, the candy counter, the pop-corn machine. Well, you know children. I'm sure I'll be able to find him. Thank you. It won't take a minute.

(*To herself*) Why, she looked at me as though I were a thief. It's getting so nobody trusts anybody at all these days.

Look at that poster. "Kiddie Matinee Today. The Monster Walks Again and Revenge of the Vampire. Special Added Attraction: Chapter Five—The Headless

Corpse." Now, how could anybody sit through such things? Well, it's for the children, I suppose. (*Turns head as if to speak to another person*)

No, I don't have a ticket, young man. I've just explained everything to the girl outside. My son, yes—I must get him at once. The Berrys are coming tonight and you know how they are. Oh, you don't? Well, there are so many things to do, and little Albert—yes, the movies. . . . You're very kind. Have you seen him, by any chance? About so high, with reddish hair? . . . .Yes, a few freckles and a tee-shirt. You've seen hundreds of them? No, I suppose it's hard to remember *every* child. But my Albert—(*Breaks off and looks around, surprised*)

He's gone. Well, I've come this far. Now for the extreme right row and—oh, I can't see a thing. And listen to that din! It's like a boiler factory! If I walk along carefully and grope, I might—(*Feeling her way*)

Oh, I'm sorry, sir. I didn't realize that was your head. My mistake. (*Looking towards screen*)

Heavens, look at that terrible thing on the screen. Climbing through the window—all green and mouldy and—that poor girl! She doesn't see him. Oh, turn around —do something!

Listen to those children. Bless their poor terrified little hearts. The thing is coming closer—closer—closer! He— it's wrapping its fingers around the girl's throat. And how realistic. I wonder how those movie people create that spurting blood.

Oh, oh! Someone's at the door. The hero. He must be the hero with that wavy hair and technicolor eyes and things. Oh, he's going to save the girl. The monster is escaping through the window!

Now the children are groaning. It almost seems as though they're disappointed. But I must be wrong. Perhaps they're sighing with relief. (*Looking away in disgust*)

Such pictures are disgraceful. I'll remember to speak about such goings-on at the next P.T.A. meeting. Poor little Albert. Just terrified! Oh, the P. T. A. must do something about monsters—and things! (*Stepping over someone*)

I'm sorry, madam, but I'd like to get through the aisle. No, I will *not* sit down. I'm looking for Albert and I think he's over there. . . . Your shoes? No, I did not kick them. Well, if you kept them on your feet—(*To herself*)

Takes up the *entire* aisle. You'd think that some people would have more important things to do on a Saturday afternoon. (*Louder to another usher*)

Please stop shining that flashlight in my eyes, young man. No, I do not have a ticket and we've gone into that before. It's little Albert. Yes, I'm sure he's sitting over there. Please lend me the flashlight. Now, if I can get his attention and—oh, I'm so sorry, sir. I didn't mean to shine it in your eyes. Your head—it looked a little like Albert's. Yes, I can see now. It's much bigger, of course.

Oh, here's your flashlight, young man. I'll find Albert myself. And I wish everyone would stop shouting about my sitting down! (*To herself*)

Such insolence! I'll try that row. (*Abruptly*) Oh, I didn't see you, little boy. You spilled your soda all over that poor man? It was an accident. Here's a handkerchief, sir. Yes, things *will* happen, you know. (*To herself*)

I've never been so embarrassed. That Albert! How could he sit through this show for five hours? It must be some inherited trait—from his father's side of the family, of course. Such confusion!

(*Turns head*) What, young man? I'm not allowed to sit in the kiddie section? Don't be foolish. Just one minute. (*Loudly*) Oh, Albert, there you are! No protests—you're coming home right now. Stop screaming and yelling like that. Just wait until I get you outside where I can see.

Albert, please stop making such a fuss. Now, young man, you march right up this aisle and behave yourself. (*Turning to speak to someone else.*) No, sir, I do not appreciate your comments. Spoiled? My child is perfectly normal and—let go of that man's hair, Albert!

The lobby at last! Now, young man, I'll teach you to—

(*Suddenly*) But how could I have made such a mistake? Your tee-shirt and red hair and all. No, sonny, it's mistaken identity, that's all. You can go back and watch the picture. Stop screaming! Kidnap you? What a perfectly ridiculous idea! All right, here's a dime. No, I am *not* the Monster Woman! (*To herself*)

Now, what am I going to do? Well, that dreadful child is gone, anyway. I suppose there's nothing else left except to go back and look for Albert. I've tried every other aisle. I suppose I might as well look down here.

Oh, oh. That thing is back on the screen. That poor girl! How could the hero have been so thoughtless, letting her go traipsing around a graveyard—alone? Really, the girl must have needed a transfusion after making that picture! (*Bends down as if to speak to a child*)

No, I don't work here, little boy. Yes, it's right over

there. The door with the little red sign. Don't you know how to read? I don't know what they teach children today. Can't even make out a simple, three-letter word. Oh, the P.-T.A. will hear about that, too.

Of course not, sonny. I can't go in *there* with you. Well, ask the usher, then. (*Suddenly recognizing another person*)

Oh, Mr. Jamieson—how nice! You're looking for your children, too? I'm afraid that I'm at the end of my rope. . . . What? What? No, I can't hear a word with this racket. Yes, the monster—he's evidently after that poor little girl again. Oh, you found your son? Hello, Billy. Yes, I'm looking for Albert.

What? He's not here! The Strand—oh, no!

Oh, Albert didn't want to see this picture? What? "The Horror Men on the Moon" and "The Creature of the Pit"? Yes, I suppose Albert would find them more appealing. But I distinctly told him the Orpheum and— why, yes, Mr. Jamieson, I'd certainly appreciate it if you'd drive me over there. (*Turning to speak to another woman.*)

Oh, madam, so you missed the end of the picture. Well, I am sorry. I didn't mean to block your view but my little Albert and—oh, so what? After all, you'll be able to see it on the late, late, late show in a couple of years.

Yes, Mr. Jamieson. I'm coming right along. (*She exits quickly.*)

THE END

15

Home Movies

> GEORGE TOLLIVER, *a middle-aged subur-*
> *banite, stands in the center of the room. The*
> *scene is the living room of the Tolliver*
> *home. There is a table downstage, and there*
> *may be a movie projector on the table, if*
> *desired.* GEORGE *smiles a warm greeting.*

Come on in, folks. Glad to see you again. (*He turns and calls.*) Eleanor! Mary and Fred Johnson are here. . . . What? . . . Oh, leave the dishes until tomorrow. This is really important! (*He walks downstage and stands proudly at table.*) Yep, that's right, Fred—I took some movies again. Color, too! . . . Oh, yeah, about three rolls. Oh, this picture is *much* longer than the last one. . . . Well, Mary, you'll have time to see all the pictures. We'll have the film spinning in a minute. Snap off the lights, Eleanor! Hah! Hah! When bigger and better pictures are made, George Tolliver will make 'em!

"Our Trip to Niagara Falls"! Yes, I stenciled the titles myself. Oh, it's a real professional job, all right. Well, there are a few rough spots—but even those guys in Hollywood make mistakes.

There's the highway. . . . Early morning? No, I shot these pictures around lunch time. Yes, overexposed, I guess, but if you squint real hard, you can follow the road and—

That dratted film! It split again. Oh, well, we'll have it together in a minute. (*He works on film.*) You know, it's the little setbacks that make home movies so much fun. You never know what you're going to get.

And—there are the falls! Ah, the full beauty of nature captured on the film and—what, Mary? (*He squints.*) You're right! The water is flowing *up!* I—I must have spliced the film upside down. Well, I'll fix that in a minute.

(*He reads.*) "Cousin Emma's Wedding." That's the next one. . . . What, Fred? What happened to Niagara Falls? Yes, yes, I took more pictures, but they didn't turn out too well. . . . Yes, I'm sure that the fellows at the developing plant must have done something to the prints. Oh, they're going to hear from me, all right!

Now, there's the whole family outside the church. Uncle Jonathan—Aunt Mary—yes, the one with the nose. Cousin Walter . . . Bill . . . Gabe and— Oh, you don't know Eleanor's relatives? Well, they're a great bunch and this is a dandy time to get acquainted. I always said that home movies bring folks together with people they've never met before.

Oh, get this! The bridal couple is leaving the church.

Yes, Eleanor took these pictures. Now, isn't that a beautiful scene and—what? (*He speaks sharply.*) Eleanor, I told you to keep your camera focused on the bridal couple. Yes, well how did that fish truck get into the picture? Yeah, the guy's holding up a codfish. . . . Oh, the camera slipped?

Fred, I'm warning you. You'd better keep the little woman away from your camera. Yes, things happen like that all the time. (*Sourly*) A fish truck! Eleanor, how could you?

Well, folks, here's the reception. Wow! What a time! (*Proudly*) I took *these* pictures. (*He looks scornfully at Eleanor.*) Now, isn't that something? Cousin Emma is feeding the groom a piece of wedding cake. Oh, I go for the "homey" shots, all right. And was that girl nervous! Look, she practically pushed the groom's face into the cake. That brought down the house and—

Just a minute, folks. The film's broken again! (*He fumbles with the projector and repairs the film.*)

Yes, Fred. Overexposed. The lighting at the reception was pretty terrible. Well, if you look hard you can see the backs of the guests. (*He waves excitedly.*) And there's Aunt Clarissa's little girl. You should have heard the laughs when she poured hot coffee into the trombone. What a mess!

That's the end of the wedding pictures. (*Suddenly*) But, you can't leave yet, Fred. Why, I haven't shown you the best pictures. . . . Heck, Eleanor, the Johnsons are interested in home photography. Why should they be bored? I—I spent five hundred bucks on this set-up and everybody likes pictures. Why, this is much better than sitting glued to a TV set and— (*He bends over projector.*)

Help! Help! Get a knife—or something. My tie's caught on the projection reel and—*help!* (*He stands and rubs his neck tenderly.*)

Thanks, Fred. Oh, no, my neck doesn't hurt much! Yes, yes, we'll get back to the movies as soon as I unwind my tie! (*He makes several adjustments.*)

There! Everything's in running shape again. (*He reads title.*)

"The Tollivers at Home." Now, this is my favorite picture. The family! There's nothing like it, Fred. Why, if everyone enjoyed family life, there'd be less juvenile delinquency and—oh, that! Well, Eleanor and I were having a little argument and Herbie got out the camera. . . . (*Uneasily*) Yes, he's quite a cameraman. Yes, quite! You— you can read Eleanor's lips and—she didn't say *that!* I'll have you know my wife doesn't use such language!

Now, this is little Ellie's third birthday party. Look at those kids! I'll never forget that shot. One of the kids threw a soda bottle, and—yes, fifty bucks for a new lens. (*Sighs*) Oh, well, it's still the family!

What's that, Fred? (*He straightens.*) Gee, I don't know. Eleanor, is something still cooking on the kitchen stove? Nothing? Then what do I smell and—water, *quick!*

Yes, yes, it's the film! Be careful with that water, Fred. What do I care about the old drapes? I don't want the projection motor to get wet. . . . Call the fire department? Don't be silly, Eleanor. (*Sadly*) And I guess that's the end of "The Tollivers at Home."

I don't know. It—it never happened before. . . . Eleanor, I didn't like that remark. I should know how to run my own projector and— (*Hopefully*)—maybe the film's not completely ruined. Let's see if it will run through and —*yes!* Ah, there's a picture. (*He frowns.*)

But I don't remember taking that one. (*He squints*) Why, it looks like—it *is*—it's you, Eleanor. That's the time you gave yourself a mudpack—and a home permanent. . . .

Eleanor, I simply don't know a thing about that picture. Besides, we're all friends and—stop crying! Well, Herbie must have been at the camera again. And—what are you doing, Eleanor? Why, you can't put the projector away, just like—*that*. The Johnsons want to see more pictures.

What? Oh, you mustn't leave, folks. Then—then come again. Yes, real soon. Yes, more home movies. (*He nods.*) Goodbye.

Now, don't start in, Eleanor. It's not my fault Junior took that picture. (*He calls sweetly.*) Oh, Junior . . . come on downstairs, son. . . . You and Daddy are going to have a little heart-to-heart talk! (*He rolls up his sleeve and grimaces threateningly.*)

THE END

16

Visiting Hours

> MRS. ACKERMAN, *a flighty, talkative wo-man, enters. The scene is a private room at the city hospital.*

My dear Emma! I came the minute I heard about your nasty accident. The very minute! How well you're looking —er—I'm sure you *must* be looking well underneath all those horrid old bandages. . . . Let me see. (*She peers intently.*) Oh, yes—there's your nose. Well, that's still in place. Ha, ha! Oh, you know me—Little Miss Sunshine. Always making a joke. I'll cheer you up, all right! . . .

What's that, dear? It's so hard to understand you with all those muffly things around your mouth. Oh, yes—of course . . . down the cellar stairs. All twelve steps! My, that sounds bad. Well, you'll be up and around in no time. As good as new, darling. (*She gasps.*) Why, those are the very words I said to Mrs. Nicholson. . . .

Oh, you must remember her. Now, let me see—you

probably moved to town *after* her accident. Yes, a cellar fall. I visited her at the hospital shortly before—before— (*She dabs at her eyes.*) Oh, it was the nicest funeral!

Now, don't think about such things, Emma. Really, we must do something with your spirits. Here—perhaps you'd like to sit up. I'll just crank the bed a few times and— (*She bends and cranks hospital bed.*)

Gracious, Emma—your leg—yes, the one in that funny splint—it's going up in the air! . . . The wrong crank? How foolish of me! Well, we'll fix that. I'll just turn the crank back. (*She cranks.*)

Just look at you—you naughty girl! Your head is hanging over the top of the bed. Oh, dear—the wrong crank again! I'll never understand these complicated hospital beds. Here—this must be the right one. (*She turns another crank.*)

Now, that's better. . . . Your leg? Well, it was *up* in the air when I got here. Oh, no, I don't think it's any higher now, dear. Well, perhaps it will be good for the circulation or something.

Oh, gracious, I could find my way around this place blindfolded. Yes, indeed. No, I've never been a patient here. I like the Westfield hospital better . . . Well, there are stories, Emma dear, but I wouldn't worry. Oh, you'll get good care, I'm sure. . . .

Oh—lunch time! My, look at that nice tray. Now, with all this good nourishment, you'll be right as rain and— vanilla pudding! My favorite dessert. Oh, Emma, it's *your* lunch. . . . Well, maybe I'll just nibble around the edges.

Oh, this pudding will do you so much good. . . . Yes,

it *is* delicious. Well, one more spoonful—but I want you to enjoy it. . . . Yes, I think I'll sit here on the edge of the bed. Now, you forget that I'm here and eat that delicious food.

I suppose you've had many visitors. And that nice husband of yours is here every night . . . Oh—he had a meeting last night? He didn't visit you? What a shame! Well, I suppose he's having a terrible time these days—getting the house all fixed up after the storm. . . . Oh, your husband didn't tell you? Well, there wasn't much water in your basement—he probably didn't want to bother you about it. Of course, it was a shame the way that big maple crashed into your dining room window but—oh, he didn't say anything about that, either?

Emma, are you comfortable? You're squirming so! It's just as I've always said. This hospital—there's never a nurse around when you need one. One could lie here forever without any attention. . . . Oh, Emma, I don't really know what happened to your dining room. You'd better ask your husband. . . .

Now, Emma, I've saved you one nice spoonful of your vanilla pudding. . . . You don't care for any? Oh, dear, I'm so sorry. But if you're sure you don't want it, I'll just finish it off. . . . What? I might as well eat your salad, too? And drink your coffee? Why, Emma dear, what's the matter? Don't you feel well? Would you like the nurse? No, I suppose she wouldn't bother to answer the buzzer, anyway. Why, it was the same way when Mrs. Nicholson was a patient. . . .

Oh, yes—in this very hospital. She looked so peaceful

the last time I saw her. . . . Now, take your mind off those things, Emma. You're going to be perfectly all right. . . .

But you *shouldn't* worry about things at home. Why, I heard the fire department got everything under control in no time. . . . What? Well, your husband probably forgot to tell you, there was so much excitement. . . .

How ridiculous! How could you possibly leave the hospital in your condition? Oh, I know you're restless—poor dear—but Jim will take care of things. I'm sure of that. . . .

A little water? Yes, of course. The jar on the table. Just depend on me. Little Miss Helpful! Would you like me to crank the bed and—

All right, Emma. I won't touch the crank. Mercy, you're so jumpy today. Hospital nerves, I call it. I'll just prop up your head and give you the water. (*She pours water and offers it to the patient.*)

Now, isn't that refreshing? It does one so much good and— Emma! Emma! What's the matter, dear? The what? Oh dear me—the water your flowers were in. But what was it doing on your table without the flowers in it. Naturally I thought it was your drinking water. Don't swallow it—oh dear, you already have! Wait, I'll ring for the nurse. Please don't look that dreadful sick way— (*She looks up, startled.*)

Oh, nurse! Something's wrong with your patient. . . . Oh, you think she needs a little rest? Well, perhaps. But she was enjoying my visit so. . . .

Never mind, Emma. I'll come again tomorrow. Now, you just rest and don't worry about a thing. I'm going right over to the police station now to find out if they got your curtains back yet. . . .

Now, not another word, dear! Just keep quiet and rest. Goodbye, dear. And remember—*be cheerful! (She goes out.)*

THE END

17

It's a Mystery to Me

&∾§§∾&

> Tom Hopkins *sits typing at a desk down center. A large dictionary and pages of a manuscript are on the desk.* Tom *types for a moment, then stops, clucks in exasperation, and looks up. The scene is the Hopkins living room.*

Is that necessary, Lois? Yes, I mean the vacuum cleaner. (*He pats the typewriter affectionately.*) This is much more important. I was right smack in the middle of murdering Lord Abernathy and—spring housecleaning? Look. . . . His Lordship is lying in a pool of blood on the manor floor—messing up the place—and you're worried about *our* drapes!

What do you mean—why can't I be like a salesman, a truck driver, an insurance man? We've gone over that before. (*He sighs impatiently.*) Yes, I quit my job at the advertising agency. . . . Why? Because I want to write

95

something on my own—something really good! (*Picks up script and waves it enthusiastically*) Listen, this isn't bad at all. You take this old goat, Lord Abernathy, and you put him in a musty, cobwebby manor and—

For Pete's sake, quit bawling! You're dripping on my script. No, I have not been fired. I *left* my job. . . . We're *not* going to starve! For ten years, I've written copy about Peter's Pickles and Lady Macbeth Wrinkle Cream and I'm fed up with the whole set-up. How creative can a guy get about a jar of pickles?

Please kids, stay out of here! Oh, you'll get your dress for the prom, Sally. I'm not *that* broke—*yet!* And we're *not* going to move into an attic, Junior. Whatever gave you that idea?

Now, clear out! (*He smiles, relaxes and resumes typing. After a moment, he looks up in exasperation.*)

Oh, Lois—will you get the door? Lois! Lois! (*He rises and pushes chair back.*) There's never anyone around when the doorbell rings. (*He walks right and opens door.*) Oh, hello, Mrs. Aspley. Mrs. Philpotts . . . how are you? (*Grimly*) So nice of you ladies to drop in. . . . Lois? Oh, I guess she's out in the garden— Oh, you'd like to give her that rosebush? Fine, she'll like that. Yes, just put it down.

Oh, yes, I'm doing a little writing. (*He touches the typewriter.*) You—you heard that I gave up my job to become a writer? Lois told you at the club meeting last week? Oh, news certainly gets around!

A speech? Me? Well, I don't know. You see, I'm not an established writer and I don't know what I could say to the ladies at the club meeting. . . . You've outlined a subject for me? Symbolism in modern poetry? Why, I don't know any more about that than I would about the tsetse fly. No—I'm sorry, but I really can't do it. . . . Yes, Lois is out there—in the garden. . . . This way, ladies. (*He follows them to exit.*) Meddlesome old hags!

(*He returns to desk.*) Now, why do people think a writer can discuss anything from the inner construction of an igloo to the South American diet? (*He sits, gives a loud scream of pain, and rises quickly, rubbing the seat of his trousers.*)

(*Turning*) Yes, Mrs. Philpotts—I found your rosebush —on *my* chair! (*He touches trousers delicately.*) No—not at all. I'll be all right. No, I won't need any first aid! Goodbye! (*His lips move wordlessly as she exits. He sits, carefully. He resumes typing but looks up shortly.*)

Oh, no—not the doorbell again! (*Sighing, he answers the door.*)

Yes, I'm Mr. Hopkins. . . . You're the carpenter? Do we need a carpenter? . . . What? You're going to build a bookcase for us? *Where* are you going to build a bookcase? (*Nods sadly*) In *this* room. (*He calls loudly.*) Lois! Lois! Ah, there you are—well, tell this guy we don't need a carpenter. He thinks that he's going to build a bookcase in this room. . . . Oh, you hired him? The bookcase—a surprise for my birthday? Well, that's very sweet, but I've waited five years for a bookcase and couldn't I finish my story first? After all, Lord Abernathy is still in that pool of blood.

Well, I don't care whether the carpenter's staring at me or not. If I want Lord Abernathy in a pool of blood, that's my business! And . . . don't start crying again. All right, let him build the bookcase. (*Defiantly*) See if I care!

(He returns to desk and resumes typing. His fingers pound the keys violently and his head moves as though keeping in rhythm with the carpenter's hammering. Finally, he shakes his head.)

Hey, bud—can't you hammer a little more quietly? . . . Oh, you don't have any rubber-headed hammers! Hah! Hah! You're a comedian, all right. *(He continues to type, but it is obvious that the noise is driving him to distraction. Finally, he rises and shoves his hands into his pockets.)*

Look, buddy, how much are you charging my wife for that bookcase? Eighty dollars? All right. . . .I'll give you one hundred dollars to get out. Never mind about the bookcase. If I don't get finished with Lord Abernathy, I'll have to move, anyway. . . . Yes, please leave me alone! What? The body? What are you talking about? The fellow in the pool of blood? No, I don't have him in the house. . . . Goodbye! *(He wipes brow, returns to desk and continues typing vigorously. Suddenly he puts his head on top of the typewriter and sobs hysterically.)*

The—the doorbell. *(Weakly)*—Lois, it's the doorbell again. A conspiracy! Yes, that's what it is—a conspiracy against my writing. *(He answers door.)*

Oh, hello, kids. . . . Yes, Sally's around somewhere. . . . What? You're having a meeting here? You can't! . . . Oh, it's Sally's turn to entertain the club and—what? Twenty-five teen-agers? *(He turns.)* Yes, Sally, some of your friends are here. . . . Oh, no—just about every kid in town.

Well, Sally, I don't care whether it's your civic duty or not. They're going out into the garden—every last one of them. . . . Yes, you kids will love it out in the garden.

There's sunshine and everything that goes with it. . . . Put that script down! Oh, you don't like that jazzy stuff? Well, let me tell you something. It's a pretty good story and— They're gone. (*He looks off left and shrugs, then returns to desk and resumes typing. Suddenly, he turns towards the door.*) The doorbell! (*He scoops up the script and waves it wildly.*) Hah! Hah! The doorbell! (*He rises, upsetting his chair. He tears the script into small pieces and scatters them around the room. He dances wildly, tearing at his hair and sobbing loudly. Finally, he stops at the desk, picks up a large dictionary and approaches the door. As he opens the door, he raises the dictionary threateningly above his head. Suddenly, his manner changes and he smiles weakly.*)

Oh, oh—hello, Officer. It's a lovely day. (*He quickly places dictionary on desk.*) And how can I help the police?

What? . . . A warrant for my arrest? But there must be some mistake—and what are the charges?

Suspicion of—murder? The carpenter? He—he told you that I had killed a man and had him lying in a pool of blood! (*Weakly*) Hah! Hah! Oh, is that all? Why, I do that all the time and—put those handcuffs away!

(*Quickly*) But I—I'm a writer, I think. Yes, Lord Abernathy—he's a character in my story. . . . No, I am *not* a character. Here, read the thing for yourself. The script— oh, the script. (*He drops to his knees and frantically scoops up pieces of the torn script. As he salvages a handful, he throws it in the direction of the policeman.*) You see, it's all a mistake. Kill anyone? Why, do I look the type—I *do*? But I'll show you that you're wrong.

(He quickly gets to his feet as though assisted.) Police headquarters? But—but I wouldn't kill anyone. I—I—I love people. At least, I did before this morning. *(He moves as though pushed towards the door.)* Oh, Lois! **Lois!** *(He shouts hoarsely.)* Oh, Lois! *(He exits quickly.)*

THE END

18

Opening Night

❦

Miss Althea Peet *enters right, waving a play script. The scene is backstage at the Lazy Daze Amateur Theatrical Company's performance of "Macbeth".*

All right, all right—curtain in five minutes. Margaret, have you seen the audience? Yes, the place is filled and I saw several of them smiling. Well, they *look* alive. That's something. Oh, an opening night does strange things to me. It's warm, brilliant, invigorating. I—I feel exhilarated! . . .

Indigestion? Margaret, how un-theatrical! I've directed the Lazy Daze Amateur Theatrical Company for three years but this is our most ambitious production. *Macbeth!*

Places, everyone. Margaret, who is that child? Yes, the unpleasant-looking little girl with the carrot hair. . . . Mrs. Kensington's daughter? No baby-sitter? Well, really —if that isn't like Mrs. Kensington! . . . Yes, see that

101

she keeps out of trouble. If some women refuse to hire baby-sitters, they should forget dramatics.

No, little girl—put down that spear!

Oh, Mr. Harwin, I hope she didn't hurt you. . . . Your costume? Well, if you keep facing the audience, perhaps no one will notice it.

Where is Lady Mac—er—Mrs. Felton? Well, ask her to get on stage. Temperamental! . . . I know, Margaret, it happens every spring. Oh, a veritable Bernhardt! For a night, at least.

Now, our witches. Where are the witches? . . . Oh, yes, of course. I didn't recognize you without your masks. Where are the witches' masks? Locked in the prop room trunk? Well, get Mr. Landers. He's in charge of such things. . . . Oh! In Poughkeepsie—his mother-in-law's lumbago? He shouldn't have taken the key. What are we going to do with your faces, ladies? Never mind. Perhaps the audience won't notice.

Mr. Peabody, are you ready with the lights? That man. Color-blind! Why was he put on the lighting committee, anyway? . . . I know, Margaret—no one *ever* wants the lighting job.

Oh, there are so many things to remember at the last minute. I'm prepared this year. Yes, I made a little list. Now, let me see.

(*She reads list.*) Mr. Grayson—upstage right, slowly to the left. Now, what does that mean? Oh, yes. Mr. Grayson, remember to let the audience see your *right* profile—but cock your head to the left. Yes, that's right. (*Whispers*) He has a good profile, really, if one has a certain seat in the audience.

Mr. Tolliver, our Macduff, less gusto. Yes, with the sword. We can't have another accident. Yes, yes—at least six inches from Mr. Grayson's face. No, no, Mr. Grayson—it's barely noticeable with the grease paint and all.

And another thing— Oh, what's that commotion in the audience? Mrs. Kensington's little girl—walking in front of the curtain! Get her in here at once. She'll ruin the mood. . . . You can't reach her? Well, use the end of the spear. Yes, yes, Margaret—just a little further. There! You've hooked her. Now, give it a good yank. (*She sighs.*) Child, you must be seated!

No, Mrs. Rainier, I don't think that a vocal rendition by your great-aunt during intermission is advisable. Oh, I know she has a good voice and all but—well, what would Shakespeare think? Some other year, perhaps.

Honestly, Margaret, her *great*-aunt. Everybody wants to get into the act!

And the courtiers—you must enter and exit more quickly. Yes, yes, I realize that it's a small part but remember what Milton said. Something about standing and waiting. A little role is important even though it's a walk-on. Especially Mrs. Leonard. Yes, no smiling at the audience, if you please. You almost tripped at dress rehearsal.

Now, everyone, a moment of relaxation. Let's compose ourselves. (*She exhales heavily.*) Yes, that's right. Oh, it's wonderful at curtain time. Why, I'm as relaxed as—

Horrors, Margaret, what happened? The kettledrums? Will you please tell that child to keep seated? Gracious, I won't be the same for the rest of the night.

103

Now, what about the final set? Mr. Fellows, did you put the finishing touches on Lady Macbeth's bedchamber? Oh, wonderful. . . . What? Turquoise! I can't imagine her in a turquoise bedchamber. . . . That man, Margaret! These would-be artists will be the death of me!

(*She frowns angrily.*) Ah, Mrs. Felton, I'm so glad that you could join us and—what have you done to your costume? I hardly feel that Lady Macbeth's sleep-walking scene is the place for bikini pajamas! We must remember propriety, my dear. Yes, the P.-T.A. and all those other things.

I don't know what I'm going to do with her, Margaret. Why was she ever chosen as Lady Macbeth? . . . Yes, yes —her husband sponsors our group. . . . I understand. It's probably the only way he can get her out of the house for a few nights.

Oh, gracious! Look at Mr. Featherstone's legs! I—I didn't notice them at dress rehearsal. . . . Well, I didn't realize he was that knock-kneed. No more costume roles for him. As if I didn't have enough to worry about—now it's his legs!

Yes, I know all about your great-aunt, Mrs. Rainier. "The Star-Spangled Banner." Patriotic and all that. . . . Yes, we'll feature a specialty show next year. Oh, we couldn't manage without her, I'm sure. . . . Yes, I know that she's been rehearsing all week. Your neighbors told me all about it. . . .

Margaret, you should have heard what they said. Great-auntie—a regular lease-breaker!

Heavens, there's the overture. I told Mrs. Peck to do

something about that piano. Listen. It's out of tune. . . . The piano tuner was here this afternoon? Well, it's probably Mrs. Peck.

Dim the footlights, Mr. Peabody. Yes, the footlights. And—

I said dim the *footlights*—not the *house* lights! Gracious, the audience is in a panic. Do something, Margaret! No, not that switch. Who turned out the lights?

Ah, that's better. Thank heavens, they used torches in Macbeth's day. Isn't there anyone who knows something about switches and things? No, I didn't mean anything personal, Mr. Peabody.

Put down that torch, little girl. Watch out, Mr. Grayson. Oh, no! Your lovely beard! Quick, somebody, get a pail of water!

Oh, Mr. Grayson—your profile. A little scorched? Mrs. Kensington, you must do something about your daughter. Yes, I know she's only a curious little girl—but *what* a little girl!

I didn't say anything about her upbringing. Well, if you feel that way, Mrs. Kensington—what? Leave the cast! But that's impossible. You're our most prominent witch. . . .

Well, I never! She stormed off in a huff. She's taken the brat, at least. Two witches, ladies. It'll have to be *two* witches. . . . Yes, we'll forget Mrs. Kensington's lines. I don't think Shakespeare did very much with them, anyway.

Raise the curtain. Mr. Grayson—not so close to the curtain, please! Margaret, Margaret! Help Mr. Grayson.

His costume—it's caught in the curtain. Oh—oh—there he goes! (*She looks up at the ceiling.*)

We'll have you down in a minute, Mr. Grayson. Please smile at the audience, at least. Ah, they're lowering the curtain. Did you see those people? They must think we're stark, raving mad!

Yes, Mr. Grayson, this has been a hectic night. Well, we'll have a nice time at Mrs. Kensington's party and—goodness, I forgot! She's in charge of the refreshment committee. The food—the refreshments—everything—all at her house. . . . Yes, yes, Margaret—go after her. Bring her back. Yes, her little girl, too. Oh, the child can play Lady Macbeth, if she likes.

Never mind, Margaret. You'd better stay here—before Mr. Peabody electrocutes someone. I'll get Mrs. Kensington. Yes, in a minute. (*Gallantly*) Good luck, everybody! (*She gestures triumphantly.*) And remember— The play's the thing!

(*She exits left, calling: "Mrs. Kensington! Mrs. Kensington!"*)

THE END

19

A Case for Two Detectives

❦

QUENTIN VAN QUENTIN, *a suave detective,*
enters. He carries a magnifying glass. The
scene is a living room. An armchair is down-
stage.

Ladies and gentlemen, we are going to witness a murder.
Rather, we are concerned with the solution of the murder
because the victim has already been ·"done in". We will
not meet him, and it is small loss because I understand
he was a bit of a rotter.

Instead, we are going to present two solutions to the
crime. One solution is offered by Quentin Van Quentin,
the typical armchair detective. (*He bows courteously*.)
That's me. The other solution will be delivered by Rivets
O'Neill, the rough-and-ready private eye. You'll see him
later.

Of course, I do not agree with the blood-and-thunder
methods of the private eye, and I will now prepare to show
you how I, Quentin Van Quentin, use my superior in-

telligence to solve the case. (*He taps head significantly, and then points to the stage.*)

The setting of our play is the palatial Long Island estate of Cyrus Barton. Cyrus Barton is the victim—or rather, I should say, *was* the victim. His wife Stella Barton is sitting in his library now trying not to act too pleased because she is rid of her husband. Susan, her daughter by a former marriage, is there too—to provide the love interest, of course. Annie, the maid, is listening at the keyhole, which is where maids like Annie always listen in mystery stories, except when they're called upon from time to time to give blood-curdling screams. I come in. (*He crosses stage.*)

Now the first thing a good detective does when he arrives at the scene of a crime is to search the room. (*He drops to his knees and examines the floor closely with his magnifying glass.*) Aha! I found it. (*Looks up, annoyed.*) What's that, Mrs. Barton? . . . No, of course I haven't found the murderer. I've found my cuff link. Now. Let's get down to business.

(*He points finger dramatically.*) Why did you kill your husband, Mrs. Barton? Don't deny it. I know everything. You hated Cyrus Barton. You quarrelled with him yesterday. He threatened to cut you out of his will, as he has done many times before. So last night you met him in this room. When he insisted that he was calling his lawyer this morning, you shot him. . . . What's that, Mrs. Barton? . . . The coroner said he had been poisoned? Please, Mrs. Barton, don't confuse the issue.

(*To audience*) Ladies and gentlemen, this part of the play is known as the Red Herring. All writers use this gimmick. They wish the audience to focus suspicion on an innocent person. I might as well tell you straight off that Mrs. Barton did not murder her husband. The Red Herring is merely a device—usually successful—to help an author prolong his play. (*He turns back to Mrs. Barton.*)

What's that, Mrs. Barton? . . . Your husband's writing desk? Ah yes, of course. Here is a letter that Cyrus Barton wrote shortly before his death. It bears yesterday's date.

(*Reading*) "Dear Sir: I have heard of your intention to marry into my family." Aha—the plot thickens. That must mean you, Miss Susan. What's that? You're not his family. You're your mother's daughter by a former marriage. Excellent, better and better. Obviously we are closing in on the criminal, my dear young lady. (*Again reading from letter*) "It is my contention that you are a fortune hunter, and there is something you must know. This girl is not my daughter and—"

Aha. There we have it. The letter ends at that point. The point at which he must have been murdered. Now, you'd better tell us everything, Miss Susan. You didn't kill him, you say? Come, come now. No hysterics. Obviously Cyrus Barton was exposing you to your fiancé. Who is this man anyway? His name is Waldemere, you say. Very interesting. And of course he is planning to marry you for your money, not realizing that you won't have any money because you're not really Cyrus Barton's daughter. Very neat.

What's that, Miss Susan? If you had killed Cyrus Barton, would you be so stupid as to leave the letter on the desk where I'd find it? Please. Stop asking embarrassing questions.

Now, Mrs. Barton, what did your husband eat for dinner last night? Vichyssoise, pâté de foie gras, pheasant —ah yes, of course. The usual simple fare. And who served it to him. Annie? (*Reflects*) Yes of course, Annie . . . What's that? Annie has just come back from her vacation. Better and better. And who cleans this room? Annie. No one else is ever allowed in this room? She has the key? (*Triumphantly*) Aha! Mr. Barton had a key but he lost it. So Annie has the *only* key. Well now, let's just have Annie come in here and answer a few very pertinent questions. (*Goes upstage, flings open door, and sees Annie, who is listening*)

Aha! Eavesdropping again . . . (*Then hissing an aside at her*) No, no, no, you idiot, this isn't when you scream. Later. Later. (*Then in normal voice*) Now, Annie. It is true, isn't it, that you have the key to this room? . . . Yes. And it is also true that you unlocked the door this morning and found Mr. Barton . . . It is? Good!

(*Rubbing his hands together, using his most cajoling tone*) Now Annie, I understand you've just come back from your vacation. . . . At Coney Island, you say. And you spent your vacation with a young man, did you not? Ah—that strikes home, doesn't it, Annie? (*Points at her.*) Annie McNamarra, I hereby arrest you for the murder of Cyrus Barton! (*Waves his arms in the direction of a constable*) Constable, take the girl away. (*Hisses to Annie*) Now, you fool! Scream. (*He steps back and holds his ears, then smiles smugly*)

How did I do it, Mrs. Barton? Elementary. You see, Annie posed as Mr. Barton's daughter while she was on vacation. So Mr. Barton wasn't referring to Miss Susan in that letter, but to Annie. The young man probably called the house. Mr. Barton found out about the deception and threatened to expose Annie, so she decided to kill him while preparing that simple meal last night. She poisoned the Vichyssoise, but then she got so impatient waiting for him to die that she came in here and shot him.

What's that, Mrs. Barton? . . . You say the doors were locked? Precisely. It was that clue that told me she had killed Cyrus Barton. She thought Mr. Barton had the second key to this room. She didn't know that the key was lost while she was on vacation. After killing him, she left the room and locked the doors behind her. And when I realized the door had been locked by someone who thought there were still two keys, I knew Annie was the murderer. Ingenious, eh?

What's that, Mrs. Barton? How did I know about Annie's young man? How did I know she had told him she was Cyrus Barton's daughter? My dear lady, what a silly question. I knew it because I looked ahead and read the last pages of the script. (*He bows with a wide flourishing gesture and exits. Five shots are heard off-stage. He returns as soon as possible in his new guise as* RIVETS O'NEILL, *wearing a trench coat, with turned-up collar, slouch hat, hands in his pockets.*)

Hello. My name is Rivets O'Neill, private eye. (*He points off-stage*) Guess you just heard that shooting. Yeah, I just rubbed out the chauffeur, the gardener, the footman, the stable boy and the upstairs maid. (*Shrugs innocently*) A fellow can't be too careful these days. (*Removes his hat, tosses it carelessly onto the armchair, then swings around toward the door*)

Well, look who's here. (*Whistles*) A doll. You the one who sent for me, sister? Oh yeah, sure—you're Susan Barton. Your old man's been bumped off, huh? Stabbed, shot and poisoned. And a heavy rope around his neck. Sounds like foul play, and believe me, sister, you've come to the right hombre to get you squared away on this little case.

Now—what did your old man do? Oh yeah, sure. A scientist. Doing important secret work for the government. Atomic research. Sure, that figures. . . . What's that? He had a secret experiment set up in his lab upstairs. He was going to announce the results today. Boy, oh boy. This gets simpler and simpler. We'll clean this case up quick as a flash, baby.

Now—who knew about your old man's work? . . . His secretary, Miss Marlow. We'll have the pencil pusher come in, toots. Then you and I can be on our way. I'll take you out of this stuffy joint. We'll head for the big city, the bright lights. I'll show you how to live.

(*Turns toward door, whistles again*) Wow! Another doll. You the secretary, huh? Miss Marlow? How're ya, babe? Now tell me, toots, what did you do last night? Or on second thought, what are you doing tonight? Sure, I'm going to find the murderer, but with you around, honey, it's hard to look for somebody else. (*Swings around to face Susan*) What's that, Susan baby? . . . I should keep my mind on business? Honey, this *is* my business. Dolls.

Now, Miss Marlow, I understand Barton finished his work for the government last night. And some guy from the government was due to come here today and pick up the papers. Did he pick up the papers? . . . What? The papers have been stolen? The lab ransacked! Well, (*Rubs hands*) now we've got it. The motive. When we find the papers, we'll have the murderer.

(*Swings around as a new character enters*) Who are you? What's that? You're not talking. Well, we'll see about that. (*Points gun*) Now, shall I let you have it or are you going to talk? (*Lowers gun, folds arms smugly*) Well, that's more like it. Your name's John Smith? And what do you do around this joint—no, don't tell me. I can guess. You're the butler. And if you're the butler, of course you stole the papers and murdered Barton. Don't deny it, wise guy. I've got you covered. You might as well confess right now and get it over with. I know your type. Butlers always kill the rich old guys. What? You're rich yourself? You're not a butler. You're John Smith, the financier. O.K., I'm not proud. So *you* murdered Barton.

What's that? You were putting up the dough for his new invention? Great! So naturally you rubbed him out because you knew the invention was going to be hot stuff and you wanted all the swag for yourself. You're the killer, Smith. You hid the papers. And I know where, too. Under your wig, you phony. (*To audience*) How did I know that? Duck soup. I read the script, too.

(*To Smith*) I knew you killed Barton the minute I heard he had been stabbed, poisoned, shot and strangled. You Wall Street tycoons are very thorough. I know your type. Leave nothing to chance. So now, Smith, you're going to die too. (*Points revolver, fires.*)

What's that, Miss Marlow— I'm a fiend? Well, how do you like that? After I've been so nice to you! Well, let me tell you something else now, baby. *You* were Smith's confederate. You had the only key. You let Smith into the lab before the government guy got here. You two stole the papers and then you were going to blow town in a hurry.

Well, sorry, baby. You're not blowing town. You'll stay right here. (*Shoots her, dusts off his hands*) Now let's see, Susan honey. Anybody else? . . . What's that? There's still one butler left. Well, never mind. We'll take care of him on the way out.

What's that? You want all the stiffs in the same place. O.K., baby. You're the boss. Get him in here, and we'll rub him out. Then you and I can be on our way. (*He removes his trench coat. There is a second trench coat underneath.*) And honey— we're really going places.

THE END

20

Mother of the Bride

❧§❧

> MRS. CYRUS BLANTON, *a middle-aged wo-*
> *man, enters. She is dressed in a gown suitable*
> *for a wedding reception. Her hands flutter*
> *helplessly. The scene is the Blantons' dining*
> *room, the morning of the wedding.*

Oh, Cyrus. . . . I've looked everywhere for you. Don't
you realize that the wedding guests are due to arrive any
minute and— Oh, sampling the punch? Yes, yes, I'm sure
that the caterer took care of that. Take your sleeve out of
the punch bowl! (*She dabs at eyes.*)

My own sweet little girl! Just think, Cyrus. After today,
she'll be gone. . . . What do you mean, I wanted her to
get married? Why, the very idea! She's so young and un-
protected and—that dreadful mother of Howard's. Oh, she
has mother-in-law stamped all over her.

We'll never be ready. We'll simply never be ready. The
caviar hasn't arrived and I don't know what's delayed the

petits fours. Oh, I hope they'll look like the lovely little things I saw in *Better Homes and Gardens.* (*She turns abruptly.*)

Yes, young man—who are you? The caviar or petits fours? . . . A messenger? Well, I'll take it here. Yes, you can put it on the table with the rest of the gifts.

Really, Cyrus, did you ever see so many presents? And such lovely ones, too. What? Ninety percent useless? Oh no, Cyrus, how can you say such a thing? Why I think they're perfectly— Which one? What are you talking about, Cyrus? I don't see any ceramic umbrella holder. That! Oh Cyrus, how can you be so stupid. That is a classic Grecian vase. From my Aunt Clara. No, I know you didn't mean anything personal.

Oh! Oh! Listen to that. *Your* Cousin Cynthia is rehearsing "Oh, Promise Me" again. Honestly, Cyrus, I don't see why you didn't discourage her. . . . I don't care how much money she has. Nobody in the world is rich enough to have such an abominable voice! (*She covers her ears and winces*) That note! A five o'clock whistle.

Now, dear, I hope you're not nervous because you must remember everything that Reverend Smithers told you last night and—oh, you're nervous, all right. Why, I could see your hand shaking when I walked into this room. Now, remember, you must walk on Mary Ellen's right— or is it the left?—I simply can't remember. We—we must go over it again. Everything must be perfect, even if you are nervous. . . . *Me?* Why, I am *not* nervous! You're the nervous one. Remember that!

(*She smiles bashfully.*) Oh, do you really think so, dear? Well, I wanted to look my best for the wedding and yes—

(*She touches her hair.*) Madame La Tour did it herself.
. . . Natural? Well, I don't know. I thought it might be a
little too daring for my age. . . . Why, thank you, Cyrus.
That's very gallant of you, but we *are* mature. (*Quickly*)
But not *half* as old as his parents!

(*She titters nervously.*) No, Cyrus, Mary Ellen wouldn't
tell me a thing about the honeymoon plans. Not a word.
She received several brochures from the Poconos and one
from Hawaii, I think—but she didn't mention them to me.
No, I've already looked in her suitcase. Howard must have
the reservations and—well, I wasn't exactly spying. A
mother should know such things. (*Righteously*) After all,
she's still my little girl and she might need me. And what's
wrong with a daughter needing her mother on a honeymoon? There are always emergencies, you know.

Thank heavens, Cousin Cynthia's stopped singing.
(*Brightly*) Maybe she's lost her voice. Well, you told me
that she often gets laryngitis. Anyway, I don't think that
"Oh, Promise Me" does much for the ceremony. It—it
sounds so servile and—oh, when I think of my little girl
scrubbing and cooking and cleaning for some thankless,
young scallawag— (*She dabs at eyes.*) I know, Cyrus. We
promised we wouldn't go into that again, but it seems so
unfair. (*Sobbing*) Men are such brutes!

Oh, hello, Mrs. Merriweather—yes, yes, you're the first
to arrive. Oh, no. There's something in my eye, that's all.
Yes, I suppose you felt the same way when your Mabel ran
off and—er—got married. You didn't? You—you weren't
a *selfish* mother? Well, really, Mrs. Merriweather, I never
considered myself a—yes, the wedding will be held in the
living room.

Can you imagine the nerve of that old—calling me a selfish mother? Of course, she didn't cry when Mabel got married. Why, the whole thing was more like a clambake and—yes, she's always the first to arrive. She sent two tiny toothpick holders and she'll eat us out of house and home. Yes, she's the kind who stays for days and days to console the mother of the bride.

Oh gracious! I just hope there'll be enough food for everyone. Mary Ellen's invited more than a hundred people not counting all *his* dreadful relatives and heaven knows how many of them there'll be. And Cyrus Blanton, if you don't stop drinking that punch there certainly won't be enough of that. Sampling! Oh really, Cyrus, put down that glass. Why, the punch in that bowl has gone down at least two inches since they brought it out. No, of course I don't carry a ruler but—

Listen to that noise in the hallway! It seems as though all the wedding guests have arrived exactly at the same time. And the children! Why, they've brought the children! Now, I ask you, what are we going to do about the food? Do children eat petits fours and caviar and things? No, I hope not. (*She smiles nervously and flutters from group to group, greeting the new arrivals.*)

Mr. and Mrs. Stockton—how nice—yes, dear—you look positively lovely. Oh, I'm so happy you could bring the entire family. . . . And the Semples and the Forbushers. Yes, yes, welcome all! No, Mrs. Forbusher, I don't think it's going to rain.

Did you hear that, Cyrus? Rain! Mrs. Forbusher would think of something like that. She hasn't had a pleasant thought in years, and being married to Mr. Forbusher and all—

(*Smiling*) The Plimptons! So glad to see you. Oh, you didn't think you'd make it? A flat tire? Yes, we're delighted that you could bring all the children—

No, no, children—we mustn't touch the wedding gifts and—stop that, child.

Gracious, I'll be a perfect wreck before Reverend Smithers gets here. You—you'd better call him. Yes, you know how forgetful he is. Why, he came to the Allens' wedding three days late and—

Cousin Cynthia's started again! No, nothing will stop her now. She'll probably sing through the entire reception, too! And I don't think that the "Road to Mandalay" is appropriate for my daughter's wedding!

(*She nudges him gently.*) Look—in the doorway—Howard's folks. Please try to smile even if you don't like them. After all, they will be in the family. (*Walks graciously and extends her hand.*) Mrs. Watkins, how charming! My dear, you look positively lovely. (*She looks down at her own gown and gives a cry of surprise.*) Yes, it *is* a coincidence. No, dear, I wouldn't have you go home and change for the world! Exactly like mine—yes, even the gloves and the shoes. The Elite Shop. (*She nods glumly.*) Oh, yes, I buy there all the time.

(*She turns, panic-stricken.*) Why, Cyrus, everyone will think that we're twins. Oh, she did that purposely! What difference does it make? Oh, Cyrus, you have no feelings—no emotions. We—we can't look the same. I'll have to change immediately . . . Oh, so you and Mr. Watkins are wearing the same type tuxedo? Well, that's different and—don't be ridiculous! Who cares whether men look alike or not?

Horrors! The wedding march! We've been talking for hours and—where's the usher? I'm to be escorted—ah, young man—for heaven's sake—*take my arm!*

Oh, you're the man with the caviar? Well, take my arm, anyway. There's no time to wait for the usher and—yes, leave the canapés here.

(*As she exits, she calls instructions to Cyrus.*) Yes, Cyrus, get out on the stairs. Now we've lived here for twenty years and you can't even find the stairs. . . . And don't step on Mary Ellen's train—and remember the right—or is it the left—and for heaven's sake, stop, stop being so nervous! (*She exits hurriedly.*)

THE END

21

For Art's Sake

> MRS. HIRAM WELKES *enters, flourishing*
> *an art catalogue. The scene is an art museum*
> *in a large city.*

Well, here we are, Hiram. This is the exhibit I wanted
to see. . . . Yes, that's right. Neo-impressionistic expres-
sionists. Oh, isn't it beautiful? From the days when art
was truly in flower.

What's that? You say it certainly looks as if art has gone
to seed. Oh, dear, Hiram, isn't that just like you. So un-
gracious, when I'm devoting my entire Saturday afternoon
to trying to improve your mind. Well, what would you
be doing if you weren't here? Spending the whole day
down in that nasty old workshop of yours, dabbling
around with heaven knows which one of your little old
do-it-yourself projects. Well, today, Hiram, *I'm* going to
do it myself. I'm going to open your eyes to art.

Book? What book? Oh, this—this is a catalogue that

explains the various pictures. . . . Why do I need a book if I'm such an expert? Well, after all, Hiram, I don't claim to know everything. And besides, some of these modern things do need a little explanation. I'm afraid you wouldn't understand them at all without me here to— (*Breaks off*)

Now, look at this picture, for instance. A classic example of abstract art. Ah, I can see it all. (*Stands, staring in rapt attention at picture, her eyes half-closed*) The struggle for existence! Do you see that red fuzzy mass in the foreground? That's a soul in chaos trying to emerge from a sea of confusion. . . . *What* soggy cereal, Hiram? (*Laughs*) Oh no, dear, that's the sky. Don't you see, Hiram, the artist is trying to interpret our struggle for perfection. . . . It doesn't? Oh my, Hiram, I'm afraid you have a very long way to go. Yes, of course you can look at the catalogue and see how it describes the picture. (*Hands him catalogue*)

What? It's called "Old Woman Wrapping a Fish"? Nonsense, Hiram. You must have the wrong number. (*Grabs catalogue, looks a moment, then slams it shut*) Well, I don't care what the artist calls it. He has no soul. Or else he's nearsighted.

(*She walks to left*) Now, *here's* something. Doesn't that little boy in the picture positively speak out loud to you, Hiram? He does? Well, what does he say to you, dear? "Help get me out of this bowl of chop suey!" Oh, Hiram, I wish you wouldn't try to be funny at a time like this.

Oh, just look at that dear little pastel over there. Wouldn't that be lovely for Cynthia's room—right over the bed? Or do you think maybe beside the bureau? No, Hiram, stop worrying. I know we can't afford it. But I do get such good ideas from looking at these pictures.

That portrait, for instance. Now, how does she fix her hair like that? (*Fixes her hair*) It gives her face such a different, distinctive look.

What did you say? Both of her eyes are on one side of her nose? Oh—ha, ha—you're quite right, Hiram. Yes, that would explain it, I suppose. . . .

Oh, my, look at that one. Shocking, I'd say. Reminds you of me, Hiram? Whatever do you mean? Well, yes, I suppose I could lose a little weight—but look like that? Never! Hiram, you must try to see these pictures more objectively. Art for art's sake, you know.

And look—look over there! An artist! I wonder what he's painting. Come, let's watch him. No, of course I won't disturb him. I'll just peek over his shoulder and— (*She tiptoes cautiously.*) Such broad, masterful strokes. A genius at work! What can he be painting? (*She rises on tiptoe, studies painting, and looks crestfallen.*) Well, I must say! No, I'm afraid I made a little mistake, Hiram. Er—he's not exactly an artist—more like a sign painter. The sign—well, it says "No Smoking". (*Annoyed*) Stop laughing, Hiram. It's so difficult to tell who's an artist these days. . . .

You know what I mean. In the old days, an artist wore a smock and a beret, and looked—well, seedy. What? Now they only look seedy, you say? Oh, no, they're thin and pale and— Oh, Hiram—look over there—across the room. That woman in that dreadful hat. No, of course it's not a painting. It's Ethel. . . . Oh dear, she's seen us now.

(*Smiles sweetly*) Why hello, Ethel! It's been a long time. The last time I saw you was at the primitive music society —what? Oh, yes, I've given it up, too. I don't have time for music any more. I'm just mad for art now, aren't you?

Yes, indeed . . . a very exciting exhibit. Take this painting, for instance. (*Points*) The colors, the shapes, the sizes! Oh, you don't like it? You think the— (*Slowly*) weight of the fluid masses is over-balanced by the diagonals? The somber tones are unrelieved by the play of light from the upper left? Er—well, yes—perhaps you're right. Yes, indeed, so nice to have seen you.

(*Looks around quickly*) Hiram! Where are you? (*Walks to right*) The very idea, Hiram! If you could have heard her—all those fine phrases. She doesn't know what she's talking about. Such nerve!

Where, Hiram? You've found one you like? Oh, this dark-looking Picasso? Well, it's not bad. But the—uh— play of light, you know—from the left. It's not—well— it's just not his best work, Hiram. You wouldn't understand.

Here's a better one. Why, this is it! The very thing. The color blue in this picture—just the color for my new dress. If I could just get a little sample of it. . . . (*Extends finger*) No, of course not, Hiram. Stop holding my arm like that. I was *not* going to scratch off a bit of the paint— although it's certainly thick enough. Well, just write down the name of this painting, Hiram, and I'll have my dressmaker come in and look at it. . . . Why are you laughing? It's called what? "Herring in Repose"? I don't care. It's still such a nice shade of blue.

And wait—don't put your pencil and paper away, Hiram. I see something else here—the window treatment in this one. For our den. Write it down, Hiram. And over here—my goodness, there's so much to see! Art is so up-lifting—it gives me so many ideas! Why, I just love art!

What? How can you say that, Hiram? I don't appreciate art? I don't look at it the right way? How can you say that? Didn't I take the evening art appreciation course with Signor Wattafoni? And the morning art lecture series with Madame de Trop? And the afternoon art lessons at the "Y"?

After all, Hiram, what do you know about art? Yes, of course, you painted the bathroom and it was a nice color— and the front door was lovely, too, even if the dog did get stuck to the door and the door got stuck to the frame— but really, Hiram, that's not what anyone who knows means by art.

(*Sighs and looks up soulfully*) We mean expressiveness, feeling, the soul—all those deep things that I'm afraid may be a bit beyond you, dear. . . . What? Not beyond you at all? Why, what do you mean, Hiram? You've never expressed the least interest—. What's that?

You say you don't express interest by talking, but by doing? Doing *what*, Hiram? Painting—down in your work-shop . . . but Hiram, how could I know? You never let me go past the cellar stairway and—what? You're painting a mural? (*Squeals*) Hiram Welkes! A mural!

(*She nods and gestures as though repeating the gestures he makes*) A long, long oblong of bright red (*Shapes it in air*)—a wide block of deep mustard yellow—a purple squiggle—a small green blob—a few dashes—and circles and circles of mud-puddle brown! (*Draws enormous circles in the air*)

But Hiram, why didn't you tell me? You're a genius. Imagine—modern art in our own basement. Who needs a museum full of old paintings? Come on, Hiram dear, let's go home to our very own art gallery! (*She smiles proudly, takes his arm and leads him off.*)

THE END

22

No Experience

FRANNIE NEWTON, *a fast-talking teen-ager, bustles in. She carries a steno note-book and pencil. The scene is the office of the Diddledock Safety Pin Company. A chair is onstage.*

Did you ring, Mr. Diddledock? Yes, sir! Yes, sir! I'll take your letter right away and—Miss Prince? Oh, she's on vacation. Yes, I'm the new girl. Last week—well, it's my first job and I know you'll be pleased with my dictation because I took 100 words per minute at Central High without hardly making a mistake and my typing ran about 50 words per minute. That's not counting erasures, of course and—yes, sir. I'll sit down. (*She approaches desk.*)

Oh, I'm sorry, Mr. Diddledock. I didn't mean to bump into your desk but I didn't see the opened drawer and, yes—a blotter will get it up. I'm sorry about all that ink. Why don't you get an automatic ink dispenser and—

oh, yes sir. (*She sits rather meekly, nods and writes in notebook.*)

Excuse me, Mr. Diddledock. Was that Samuel Benton or Samuel Benson? Benson? Thank you. (*Nervous giggle*) My brother lisps, too, but everybody says he'll outgrow it.

Yes, the letter. You have an appointment in fifteen minutes? Oh, don't worry about that, Mr. Diddledock, we'll see you get there. (*She prepares to write again.*)

Ooops, there goes the pencil point. You know, I break more pencils that way. Oh, thank you. Yes, I'll take good care of your pencil.

Now, let me see. Samuel— (*She hesitates and looks at him puzzledly*)—Benton? Oh, yes—Benson! I never forget a name, almost never, anyway. 220 Quaker Drive. Gee, that's funny. My girl friend works at 218 Quaker Drive. She's a nice girl, Ginny. She got her job at the same time I did. Really, I guess I could have gone with that company, too—but it takes ten minutes longer to get to that office from my house, so I came here.

Well, gee, Mr. Diddledock—I'm glad that I took this job, too. "Dear Sir . . . in reference to your inquiry of the. . . ." Please, Mr. Diddledock. I'm still back on the "Dear Sir." Oh, yes—I'm good at shorthand, but I never remember whether I should squiggle or squaggle. (*She moves her pencil to demonstrate.*) It's very important. If you squiggle when you should squaggle, it might change the letter all around and Mr. Benson wouldn't know what you were talking about.

"There has been a slight increase in the cost of safety pins and. . . ." (*She puts down the pencil and shakes her head sadly.*) It's a shame the way everything has gone up, though I'm sure someone in your income bracket doesn't feel it. Of course, people blame the government for reckless spending and the government blames the people for reckless spending and the whole thing gets fouled—I mean—um—mixed up, and where are you then? (*Proudly*) I learned that in my Economics course. Yes, the same school where I studied shorthand.

Oh, but of course we'll be finished in plenty of time for you to get to your meeting, Mr. Diddledock. You know, you're pretty nervous. Do you think it's high blood pressure or something? Oh, yes indeed. I know all about that, too. Aunt Gussie . . . yes, she had blood pressure for years and no one could do a thing about it—not even my uncle. (*Writes as she speaks next line*) "A slight increase in the cost of. . ." (*Looks up*) Mr. Diddledock, I know you're in such a hurry and all, but I'd like to speak about increases and things. Oh, they're so important. Well, lunches and bus fares are pretty expensive and this company starts a girl out at such a low salary, and there are other expenses like going out to dinner, and—Well, Mr. Diddledock, I've been here for a whole week and the man in personnel said something about periodic increases. I've been wondering just how periodic he meant, so I thought I'd take it up with you—because in spite of all the things they say I don't mind talking to you at all. (*She smiles sweetly.*) Why, it's almost like talking to my father and, well—I'm not afraid of you just because you're the boss, and I can't believe all those terrible things that—I'm sorry, Mr. Diddledock.

Well, if you'd at least consider when the periodic increase will be. All right, I'll take it up with the personnel department. (*She picks up the pencil and resumes writing.*)

". . . Increase in the cost of safety pins, I suggest that you call the Peter Piper Supply Company. . . ." (*She rises dramatically and screams.*) Peter Piper! (*She calms down.*) I'm—I'm so sorry, Mr. Diddledock. It's that name— Peter Piper—he's my absolute favorite singer (*Sighs*), and I just got carried away. Doesn't he absolutely send you, too? (*Tearfully*) Oh, Mr. Diddledock, what a terrible thing to say! Yes—yes, I'm sure Miss Prince has already left for her vacation. Yes, the letter—

The Benson file, Mr. Diddledock? Oh, I've been filing all your mail for the past week. Yes, sir—I'll get it. (*She stands, walks left and opens bottom file drawer. As she works, she turns.*)

Yes, it's down here somewhere. On top with the B's? Oh, no—I put it down here under "U". That's right, Mr. Diddledock, under "U". Yes, yes, I know it should go under "B", but the B's were crammed and well, my girl friend's name is Ginny Burton. Burton and Benson, get it? The same initial. Well, she borrowed my umbrella last week and I knew I'd remember the "U" in umbrella so I put the Benson letter down there. Simple? (*She stands and waves the letter triumphantly.*)

Here's the letter. My filing system? Oh, filing is easy. It's like a little game— Word Association! No, I didn't file too many letters that way. Not where there was room in the regular drawers, anyway. Yes, sir—I'll always know where they are, all right. (*She returns to chair, crashes into desk.*)

Oh, the water pitcher! Here, I'll get a sponge and—(*She makes an attempt to blot the desk*) Oh, now it's all over Mr. Benson's letter.

Never mind that, you say? You want to dictate another letter? Well, all right, but we haven't finished the one to Mr. Benson yet, and I was always taught that an efficient person should finish one thing before he starts another because if he doesn't—

Yes, Mr. Diddledock, I'm ready. (*She sits and begins to write, repeating as she writes.*) "Acme Employment Agency. Dear Sir. . . ." Not so fast, Mr. Diddledock. "I wish to find an office assistant . . . young, alert. . . . Our working conditions are pleasant . . . good starting salary. . . ." (*She looks up.*) Is someone going to leave, Mr. Diddledock? You hope so? But Mr. Did—oh, yes, sir, excuse me, the letter. (*She writes.*) "She must be *quiet, reserved* and *experienced.*" (*She puts down her pencil.*)

Mr. Diddledock, you're not planning to fire Miss Prince, are you? After all, she's been with you for years and she's a pretty good worker if you like that square kind and—oh, it's not a replacement for Miss Prince? Then why do you need another office girl? Honestly, there's not enough work for two girls.

What's that? You say you're not going to employ two girls. But Mr. Diddledock, you can't mean—you don't mean—oh, please, Mr. Diddledock, I know I don't have very much experience, but if no one wants to give me any experience, how am I going to get any? And besides, I'll never be able to face Miss Grimshaw. Miss Grimshaw was my teacher at Central High. I was the best student in the class—voted most likely to succeed. So you see, Mr. Diddledock, if you fire me now, you're likely to get one of those other students who wasn't nearly as good as I was at Central High—and then you'll feel terribly sorry you didn't hang on to me while you had the chance, because by then of course it will be too late and—

What? You *will*? Oh, Mr. Diddledock, thank you so much! You're an absolute peach to let me stay. Really. I could kiss you. No—no, all right, Mr. Diddledock, I won't kiss you. I'll just sit here very quietly and finish the letter to Mr. Benson. What? Oh, you think it will be easier to telephone Mr. Benson? Well, Mr. Diddledock, I think perhaps you're right at that. Letters are the most awful waste of time.

THE END

23

The Highway Restaurant

> JOE HANEY *sits behind the steering wheel of his car, admiring the passing countryside. His body sways with the movement of the car. The scene is the Haney car, late afternoon.*

Yes, Ann, you sure were right. There's nothing like getting away from the crowded city into the great open spaces. (*Turns to speak to the children in the back seat*) Just look at those hills and trees, kids. Did you ever see anything like it? You did, Peter? Where? Oh, on Bobby Blackwood's color TV.

(*Turns right*) How do you like that, Ann? These kids have their eyes so warped by artificial things they can't appreciate real nature when they see it. Children, I tell you this is a scene no artist could paint—that valley with the little river running through it, that color over there. . . .

What's that, Gracey? You're hungry? Oh, for heaven's sakes, Gracey, we can't stop now—just when the light is at its best, and all this wonderful color— What, Betty? You're hungry, too. You want a hamburger—with mustard and relish and a chocolate milk shake and—oh, all right, then. I guess I can't hope to interest this family in anything so intangible as beauty. At least, not on an empty stomach.

(*Turns right*) What about you, Ann? Will you settle for a quick hamburger so we can still catch some of this light? You won't? A full-course dinner? Yes, I know the whole point of this outing was to get you away from the kitchen, but—oh, all right, Ann. A full-course dinner it will be— turkey, cranberry sauce and all the trimmings. Anything to keep peace.

Now, how about that place right there on the right? Looks good? What? No cars? No, I suppose it can't be very good if it has no customers—but we'd get fast service and—what, Peter? You like that place? It said fried clams. Well, I'm sorry, son, it's too late now. But the very next one on the right. . . . What, Ann? Of course you can get fried clams and a full-course dinner at the same restaurant. Why not?

What, Betty? You see a nice one coming up. All right, dear, I'll slow down . . . oh, no—no, I won't. Not *that* place. Why not? Well, I'll tell you why not, Betty. Because your old man isn't made of money. Didn't you see that doorman? In a place like that, everyone has his hand stuck out for a tip before you even park the car—*if* they let you park your own car.

Oh, look, kids. There's an advertisement for a place that

looks just perfect. "The Se-Lect Restaurant. Full-Course Dinners. Hamburgers, Fried Clams. One quarter of a mile." That's for us, huh? Suits everyone's needs. And maybe I can even get a decent cup of coffee. There it is, coming right up. What, Betty? It's all full of trucks. Well, so much the better. Everyone knows truck drivers find the best eating places on the highway—so let's go. What, Ann? You're all dressed up and you want a fancier place? (*Wearily*) Oh, all right. But I'm telling you, the next place on the—

What, Peter? You've decided that you'd rather have a pizza? Well, it's too late now. Why is it? Because you said you wanted fried clams. (*Through clenched teeth*) I know you haven't ordered fried clams yet, Peter. But I can't be expected to produce a restaurant out of nowhere that serves turkey dinners, hamburgers, milk shakes, pizzas, and fried clams. . . .What's that, Peter? You thought you just told me I don't have to find a place that serves fried clams because you've changed your mind and—oh, all right, Peter. *All right!* That will do.

No, Ann, I am not bellowing at the child but—what, Gracey? No more restaurants? You haven't seen a place in miles? You know, Ann, I think the child's right. I haven't even seen a sign. What? What native? Yes, of course I see that farmer walking along there, but what am I supposed to ask him? If he knows a restaurant that will suit this persnickety family? Oh—I see—just if he knows any restaurant at all.

(*He stops car and leans out of window.*) I beg your pardon, sir, but I wonder if you could recommend a nice restaurant near here where I could take my family. You could? Real home cooking? Sounds first-rate, sir. Yes—go along the highway for exactly half a mile. Then just past the yellow barn, turn sharp right. Yes, I've got that. . . . Then go about a mile on that road, look for a white church and turn sharp left—then straight up the hill and watch for a little dirt road on the right, just after a sign that says "Drive slow, curves ahead". Go down that dirt road until you come to an intersection with four roads. (*Mops his brow*) Take the center road and go along for another half mile—and there it is. Oh, I see. We can't miss it. Well, thank you, sir. Thank you very much. Goodbye.

(*He starts the car and drives off, speaking bitterly.*) Well, that was helpful, I must say. Why wasn't it? Because, Ann, if you think I'm going to get myself snarled up on a lot of back dirt roads a million miles from nowhere just on the recommendation of some farmer—yes, Gracey, I know—I see the yellow barn, but I'm not going to turn off the highway. I don't care how hungry you all are.

What, Gracey? You just saw a sign? Well, good for you. . . . Oh, yes—I see it now. "Do Drop Inn. One Mile. Good, Home-Cooked Food." There now, everyone. See? You always get panicky over nothing. Why don't you just leave things to your old dad and stop worrying? You ought to know I wouldn't let my family starve.

Look, Gracey, there's another sign. "Don't bother your wife with cooking. Let us do it for you! Reasonable prices. One-half mile." You see that, Ann? Now, doesn't that prove something worth having is something worth waiting for?

No, Ann, I am not speeding—it's just that all this talk about food has made me so hungry I could eat a—yes,

Betty, I see the sign. "When you're out for a little spin—
Don't forget the Do Drop Inn." Brother, we won't forget
you. One quarter of a mile to go. Start the count-down,
kids. Our goal is in sight!

There it is—see it coming up on the right? Looks great.
No cars—well, what of it? The place probably just opened
up for dinner. What sign, Betty? No, I didn't see it—but
let's not bother about that now.

(*He stops car.*) We're here! Come on, kids, pile out.
What's that, Betty? I just told you I don't care what the
sign—*what?* "Closed for the season. Will reopen May 1st."
Oh, no. No, no, no! Say it isn't so. (*Feebly*) Gracey, bring
out that package of Life Savers and toss one to a starving
father.

THE END

24

Moving Day

> MRS. MYRA EDWARDS *rushes in right, and runs over to telephone on table, downstage. She picks up receiver, dials.*

Hello, George, this is Myra. . . . Yes, I know you have an important meeting this morning. . . . Of course I realize it's your first day in a new town with a new district staff, and—yes, we're all moved into our new house. The moving men have left, and everything is in order. Well—almost everything, I suppose.

No, nothing is in place, and there have been a few mishaps. You know how irresponsible moving men are. Everything went well until Grandmother's antique dresser rolled off the moving truck and crashed into the living room wall. It actually shattered the fireplace, and then I couldn't find the new drapes, and—yes, you heard me right—completely shattered. (*Indignantly*) Well, it couldn't have been very well constructed if the stones came loose. After all, the dresser only weighs a few hundred pounds, and—yes, it left a gaping hole. (*Sighs*) Oh, you know the building materials in these new homes.

(*Brightly*) Everything will be as good as new after you've called in a few stone masons, and carpenters, and painters. Who knows? We might install a picture window where the fireplace used to be. (*Chuckles, then pauses*) Yes, I realize the picture window would face our neighbor's bathroom, but you can't have everything. (*She looks off right and calls.*)

Good morning, Mr. Courtney. Lovely morning, isn't it? (*She returns to phone.*) That was Mr. Courtney, dear—our new neighbor. He just went past the dining room window in a rowboat. He seems terribly nice. . . .(*Annoyed*) Oh, George, why must I repeat everything? You heard me the first time—in a rowboat!

Well, it's been raining frightfully all morning, and that stream that flowed near the marigold beds has been rising steadily. As a matter of fact, it's up to the front door. . . . Yes, Mr. Courtney said it happens every spring. Now we know why he keeps that rowboat in his garage.

(*In off-handed manner*) Oh, don't worry, George. I have newspapers and old rags near the front door. Mr. Courtney said the water doesn't come into the house—not too often, anyway. (*She sighs.*)

Yes, everything is terribly disorganized. I won't have this place in order for months. (*Suddenly*) And our new set of Lenox dinnerware—the service for twelve—well, it's not for twelve anymore. The mover dropped one of the boxes, and—service for six and a half (*Snaps fingers*), just like that!

By the way, we'll have to eat out tonight, dear. There's not a perishable left in the house. The refrigerator stopped running, and all our food was ruined. (*She gestures hopelessly.*) The motor fell off! . . . .How should I know how it happened? I'm not a mechanic. (*Pause*) Yes, the motor broke into pieces, right after the moving men dropped it. . . .Well, they tried to grab Grandmother's dresser as it rolled off the truck, you see, and they lost their grip on the refrigerator, and—yes, the bottom of the motor is shattered. Thank goodness it wasn't Grandmother's bottom—the dresser, I mean.

Oh, the moving men were very courteous, and when Jasper broke loose in the basement and tore the seat of one of the mover's pants, he barely complained at all. And they were very careful, George. They hardly damaged any shubbery or trees at all. (*Suddenly*)

The trees! Gracious, I almost forgot! Do you remember the giant oak tree that hung over our boundary fence? Yes, you were always afraid it might fall. Well, there's no need to worry any longer, George. (*Uneasily*) It fell! (*Quickly*) Now, don't get excited. No, it didn't do too much damage to the fence, but the tree is lying against the side of the house. No, I don't think it broke too many shingles—or slates—or windows. Not too many at all. . . .Yes, it was the rain. Mr. Courtney was very apologetic. He told me he's insured against such things. He mentioned that it might be considered an act of nature—or something—and his insurance company might be hesitant to pay, but everything will work out just fine. And Mrs. Courtney gave me a jar of her new raspberry jam. (*Smiles*) Wasn't that neighborly?

Don't worry about me, George. Arthur is helping me unpack things. Yes, you heard me—Arthur. . . .Yes, I know he was supposed to start at the new school this morning. . . . (*Annoyed*) Yes, of course he went. Promptly at eight. (*Slowly*) But he was back at nine. Something about his transcript from the last school. He might have to repeat an entire term. (*Suddenly holds receiver out from ear*)

Please, dear, calm down! You can write a letter to the board of education when you get home tonight. (*Proudly*) In your new den! (*Soberly*) But we'll have to clear out a few branches first. . . .(*Nods*) Right through the den wall.

But, of course, we won't be home tonight. There's not a thing to eat. (*Shrugs*) Come to think of it, I wouldn't be able to prepare anything, anyway—not unless the broken gas main were fixed. (*Laughs nervously*)

Gee, I forgot to tell you about the broken main, didn't I? Yes, the movers again—when they were coming up the driveway. The truck ran across the gas line and split it right in half, or so they told me. . . .Who told me? Why, the police, of course. And the men from the gas company. And the rescue squad. And the ambulance driver. . . .No, no, George. No one was hurt. I told the policeman that they should have buried their old gas main someplace else. He said that because we're the owners of the property, it's our responsibility, and he gave me something called a citation about the driveway. Yes, it might have to be re-routed, and, well, you'll hear all about it when you appear in court next week. (*She glances left.*)

Well, isn't that a coincidence, George? The same policeman is at the door. . . .No, not the door with the tree lying against it. The one without hinges. Grandmother's dresser knocked them off.

(*Concerned*) Oh, he seems terribly excited, the poor fellow. Something about having to evacuate the neighborhood. Yes, the leaking gas main. (*She sighs.*) And I haven't even begun to unpack the clothing. Yes, I'll get your suits, George. They're in the box next to the door where the water is coming in.

I really have to go now, George. I'm sure they'll figure out how to shut off the leaking gas—and I'll see you at dinnertime. Please don't worry about a single thing, and (*Sweetly*) have a nice day! (*She hangs up, rushes off right.*)

THE END